Law and Leisure
Services Management

Michael Scott LLM

Series Editor: **Brian S. Duffield**

Longman

in association with
Institute of Leisure and Amenity Management

Longman Group UK Limited
Longman House, Burnt Mill, Harlow, Essex CM20 2JE

© Longman Group UK Limited 1988

First published 1988

British Library Cataloguing in Publication Data

Scott, Michael, *1925–*
Law and leisure services management.
    1. Great Britain. Leisure services. Law
    I. Title
    344.104'9

ISBN 0-582-02192-8

Typeset by Tradeset Photosetting Ltd, Tewin Road, Welwyn Garden City, Herts
Printed and bound in Great Britain by Biddles Ltd, Guildford and King s Lynn

CONTENTS

Acknowledgements

The author gratefully acknowledges help with background material from Susan Smith, solicitor in Wandsworth, Robert Scott, solicitor in Halifax, Mrs E. McManus, lecturer at the Percival Whitley College, Halifax, and Mr E. C. Buckwell. Longman's editorial staff have been uniformly helpful. Timescale and style were, as always, assisted by my wife's leisure services. For remaining errors, the author remains responsible.

Michael Scott   Halifax
                                                                April 1988

Preface

Recent years have seen the expansion of leisure services throughout Britain, whether they are provided by institutions in the public, commercial or voluntary sectors. Such leisure facilities and services are now recognised as of critical significance in the changing social and economic structure of contemporary Britain. The effectiveness of such provision, however, lies in the hands of leisure officers and managers and it is clear that there is a need to ensure the highest level of professional support for leisure services.

The Institute of Leisure and Amenity Management (ILAM) has been in the forefront of promoting a scheme of professional education and training leading to the qualifications of the ILAM Certificate and Diploma in Leisure Management. These professional qualifications are designed to ensure that leisure managers have a sound base of education and understanding in the operational and technical aspects of day-to-day management of leisure facilities and opportunities. Similarly there is a concern to ensure a thorough knowledge and understanding of the disciplines and skills appropriate to the manager in the leisure business.

The aim of this series is not only to provide texts which will cover constituent elements in the ILAM syllabuses but also to provide for all leisure professionals the opportunities to update and improve their practice and managerial skills. In that sense they will be relevant not only to ILAM courses but also to other educational programmes leading to Higher National Diploma and Degree qualifications as well as reference sources to the working professional.

Each volume deals with a different aspect of professional activity in the leisure field. As such the texts can be used on an individual basis to enhance skills and understanding in specific aspect of the day-to-day responsibilities of leisure managers. More significantly, however, taken together, the volumes in this series will constitute an integrated support system for professional development which will enhance the efficiency of individual managers and the effectiveness of the services they provide.

This text provides an introduction to the law as it relates to leisure services. It presents a brief general survey of the law and distils the key areas which will be of concern to Leisure Managers. The author illustrates the text with 'case law' relating to the leisure field with a particular emphasis on the practical problems that managers might face.

Brian S. Duffield   Series Editor

Introduction

The leisure services have become an identifiable area of our culture and our society in recent years and this book seeks to etch out the law affecting those engaged in management in those services.

Within our legal system, this becomes a mixture of the general law which affects all activities and the specially tailored law as it provides the working rules for sports stadiums, caravan sites, National Parks, gambling and a host of other leisure pursuits and scenes.

Inevitably this involves selection and in doing this we have sought to emphasise the law as it affects staff and commercial problems, since they provide the daily climate of leisure service managers at work. We have also provided an outline of public leisure services law as it affects parks, commons, trees and caravans. Since some foundation knowledge of the dramatis personae of the English legal scene is necessary, that is the subject of Chapter 1, and Chapter 8 introduces, if only briefly, some of the other major characters who inhabit the leisure services scene.

The law described is that which applies to England and Wales; Scotland has its own law. This interlocks with English law at such rare points – employment law appeals are one of them – that it would call for a separate book to describe that scene.

No man in leisure services can work for a week without meeting the law in one form or another. Whether it be the injured spectator at the cricket match, the pop star who cancels his engagement to appear at the festival concert or the maintenance contract hiccup for one-armed bandit machines at the swimming club, the law is basic and ever present. We hope that this volume in the new series of guides for leisure services managers will alert those engaged in that busy branch of public life to problems which concern them.

1 Law in our society

THE PRINCIPLES

Main sources of law

Common law

The law consists of the rules enforced by the Courts. Some of those rules are in the form of statutes, made by Parliament. An ever decreasing number come from traditional custom. But the greatest part of our law is the body of reported decisions of our Courts. It is principles embodied in the large collection of these reports which form the basis of English Common Law.

Historically, law was developed from customs in different parts of the land. These were unified and formed into comprehensive principles of general application. This took place over a period of time when judges were sent by the king to administer the law on their travels to centres of population.

Central Courts were established in Westminster from committees of the King's Council. The Court of Exchequer, the Court of Common Pleas and the Court of King's Bench are examples. It was the judges of these Courts who became travelling judges in the eleventh and twelfth centuries. Their accumulated knowledge formed the basis of the law which was enforced and recorded. This was done first in year books, later in law reports of named lawyers and ultimately in the series of law reports as we know them today.

As distinct from Custom, which generally prevails in localities, the Common Law applies to the whole country. Some of the early cases which developed the Common Law related to trespass and debt. A man did not return animals, money or goods he had promised to return. Or he wrongfully occupied land of the claimant. Then he was taken to Court by the man he had wronged. Other cases established the essentials of an agreement, a contract as it was called, before the Courts would enforce it. This might involve looking for the use of a seal or other signs of formality and intention, in order to decide if an agreement was to be treated as a legally binding contract. As an example, when a man bought a horse for money and said he would be willing to pay more if the horse was 'lucky' for him, the Courts held the word 'lucky' to be too vague and declined to enforce an extra payment, when asked to do so by a disappointed seller.[1]

Statute law

In these days Statute law is the prime source of new law; Parliament is a great law making machine. In 1985 it made 76 Acts and in 1986, 68 Acts. Statutes and Acts are words which are used interchangeably. An Act of Parliament is final only when it has been approved in both Houses of Parliament and, thirdly, it has the Royal Assent of the monarch.

Table 1.1 illustrates the 11 stages taken by a normal Bill, on its journey to become an Act of Parliament.

Some Bills start their life in the House of Commons and some in the House of Lords. The choice of venue can depend on the controversial nature of the Bill; it can be influenced also by the amount of business each House has in hand at the time.

Public or Local Acts

We have referred so far to Acts of Parliament. These however are of two sorts. They can be Public General Acts, of which the Housing Act 1985, the Sporting Events (Control of Alcohol etc) Act 1985 and the Films Act 1985 are examples. They can however also be Local and Personal Acts. In 1985 there were, as it happens, also 76 of these. They are, as their title indicates, limited to a locality such as the Durham City Council Act 1985 or else to a body which needs Parliamentary authority to effect some change, as the Royal Holloway and Bedford New College Act 1985, or the Streatham Park Cemetery Act 1985. These Local and Personal Acts follow the same procedure of three readings in each House, followed by the Royal Assent, as we have described for the Public and General Acts.

Case law

We have said that reports of court decisions form an important source of our law. There are several refinements that can be made to that statement and it will be useful to deal with three of the most important here.

When is a case a precedent?

A report is a source of law when it is accepted as a precedent for the application of some legal principle. (A precedent in this sense is an earlier case which a later court must take into account.) For instance, three years ago a judge found that Mr A's actions amounted to nuisance and Mr B has done the same thing today. Then today's judge would hold Mr B liable in nuisance too; he follows the earlier judge's decision because the facts of the two cases are so similar.

We give this example and emphasise that courts do not pile precedent

Table 1.1 Progress of a Bill

Order	House of Commons Stage	Action
1	1st reading	a formal publication
2	2nd reading	an explanation of the purpose and debate of the principles involved
3	committee stage	a minute examination of the text and decisions on all amendments
4	report stage	the House looks at the Bill in its revised stage after the Committee amendments and agrees or disagrees with them
5	3rd reading	the House takes a final decision on the Bill as it has emerged after this treatment

Order	House of Lords Stage	Action
6	1st reading	
7	2nd reading	
8	committee stage	exactly as in the first House
9	report stage	
10	3rd reading	
11	If both Houses agree then Royal Assent is reached, whereby the Bill becomes an Act. (If the Houses disagree then a special procedure is used to resolve the dispute.)	

upon precedent, like stooks in a haystack. Only when a clear principle of law is embodied in a decision does it stand as a precedent.

We shall be referring to text books a little later and they illustrate a further point. This is that some precedents are called persuasive and some are binding. If binding, the precedent must be followed; the persuasive authority or precedent has not that compelling nature but it is one to which respect is paid.

Ratio decidendi

This leads to the second point. The principle of law embodied in a Court's decision is called the *ratio decidendi* ie the legal principle behind the decision. A matter touched on but not crucial to the decision is an *obiter dictum* ie a thing said by the way.

Let us take an imaginary example. Recreation ground equipment was protected by a clear notice: 'No person over the age of 16 is permitted to use this equipment'. Some 18 year olds played there at night, a link on a swing snapped, being rusty and worn, and a boy broke his arm. A Court could say, if the boy sued the recreation ground owner, that he was in the same position as a trespasser and that if the owners knew that such older youths used the equipment regularly, they had some duty to do more than put up a notice eg lock the equipment with chains. To the extent that they did not do this, they were negligent.

In the circumstances the *ratio decidendi* might be: an occupier of a recreation ground does not discharge his legal occupier's duty to trespassing youths merely by putting up a notice prohibiting their entry. As an alternative, the *ratio* might be: an owner of equipment which can cause injury if misused must take reasonable steps to prevent that misuse.

The problem might become critical if, say, during a dance in a hired room in a sports centre at the other end of England, mischievous youths went wrongfully into a multi-gym next door, whilst allegedly looking for the toilets, dropped a weight on someone's foot and caused serious injury. Was there a relevant principle in the recreation ground case to be applied if the injured dancer sued the owner of the sports centre?

Again, if the Court in the recreational equipment case relating to the swings had said, during their judgement, 'Any owner of recreational equipment available for public use must be aware that mischievous youths will be enticed to use it' – would that be fundamental to their decision and part of the *ratio* or is it just an *obiter dictum*, which can be nodded to and then ignored?

Hierarchy of the Courts

Not only does a Court, when hearing a case, consider if there is relevant precedent, in the form that we have described, it also takes account of the status of the Court which created that precedent. The hierarchy of the Courts is shown in Figure 1.1.

Figure 1.1   Hierarchy of the Courts

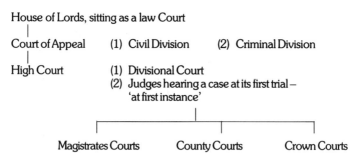

House of Lords, sitting as a law Court
|
Court of Appeal   (1) Civil Division   (2) Criminal Division
|
High Court   (1) Divisional Court
                         (2) Judges hearing a case at its first trial –
                              'at first instance'

Magistrates Courts   County Courts   Crown Courts

The normal rule is that each Court is obliged to follow a precedent set by a Court above it in this hierarchy. The language used is that Courts are bound by precedents of superior Courts. With regard to other Courts, their decisions may be treated as having persuasive though not binding authority.

We should emphasise that there are refinements about this matter which need not detain us at the moment.

Finally, when handling matters of European Community law, all Courts, even the House of Lords, must follow a decision of the European Court of Justice.

Custom

This is still a good source of law, though rare in our society. In the case of *New Windsor Corporation v Mellor*,[2] an 81 year old lady established the right of local inhabitants to enjoy lawful sports and pastimes on land in their town. It was a right, based on custom, going back 1000 years and the Court talked of maypole dancing and archery in a colourful judgement. The upshot was that the local authority was thwarted in other plans they had for the use of that land.

This sort of local custom is particular law for a particular locality. The custom upheld in the New Windsor case exhibited the four features looked for before the Courts will give legal authority to a custom. They are certainty, reasonableness, an open exercise of the custom without interruption and lastly, the right age, vintage if you like. 'From time immemorial' was the phrase used by Lord Denning in the New Windsor case. The Courts have however, by long tradition, interpreted this as meaning at least from 1189 when Richard I began his reign.

The reports have many examples of legal customs eg mending nets on the foreshore, shooting fowl on certain land, erecting stalls on certain land where a fair was held on condition of paying traditional monies to the landowner. In all cases of establishing custom, reasonableness is a matter of law for the Court. Furthermore, if the custom severely infringes private rights, the cases show that the Courts look for a stronger proof of the custom.

Lesser sources of law

Subordinate legislation

Because our complex society needs many more rules and regulations, especially for detailed matters, than Parliament has time to ponder and promulgate, Acts often include powers to make subordinate legislation. This must be within the framework laid down in the parent Act, as it is sometimes called, or it can be challenged in the Courts as being *ultra vires* ie outside the powers. If that challenge is successful, the legislation in question is treated as null and void.

In practice it is Orders, Regulations and Byelaws which form the subordinate legislation most likely to be encountered by leisure service managers.

Orders and Regulations

An Order in Council is made by the Privy Council, or a nominated committee of that council, which normally means a group of ministers. One of the Employment Acts lists certain subjects to be dealt with by Orders in Council and others by Statutory Instrument, ie Regulations. The distinction is broadly between, on the one hand, giving the force of law to changes in the amounts prescribed as maxima in connection with redundancy payments for example (ie Regulations, since the subject is already covered by legislation) and, on the other hand, bringing the law into a new area, perhaps to correct some injustice (ie the Order in Council).

It has been said that there are 10,000 Regulations in force at any one time nowadays. The Health and Safety at Work etc Act 1974 has a good example of the power to make regulations in section 15. No less than 11 topics are listed, including setting out exemptions from requirements, providing for legal defences to statutory offences, as well as creating offences and repealing earlier statutory provisions. These are obviously very wide powers indeed. An example of a Regulation under another Act of interest to readers is the Forestry (Modification of Felling Restrictions) Regulations 1985. These made an important change in the law about the girth of a tree which could be felled by a person on his own land without the need for a licence. Those Regulations were made by the Forestry Commission under the Forestry Act 1967 sections 9 and 32.

Byelaws

Byelaws, on the other hand, are a comparatively minor form of legislation. A major statute like the Open Spaces Act 1906 includes power for a local authority which manages an open space to regulate its use by byelaws. These then deal with admission charges, keeping order, avoiding nuisances as well as fixing fines for offences.

If the legal powers under which byelaws are made should be exceeded then, like Regulations, they may be challenged and possibly declared *ultra vires* in the Courts.

Text books

It is not very common to find a Court which is asked to settle an awkward piece of law, referring in its judgement to a legal text book. However such writings are often referred to in argument before the Court and so it occasionally does happen that the Courts refer to passages which are relevant.

In a wartime case where a new legal point was considered about injury to employees in an explosives factory, the House of Lords referred not only to an article in the *Cambridge Law Journal* but also to a law book on Torts.

When so used, text books are of persuasive authority; they carry no intrinsic authority: it is the judgement of the Court that alone bears that character.

Equity

In olden days in this country the law developed slowly as described earlier. Equity was the name given to the principles accepted in the Court of the Lord Chancellor, the Court of Chancery, to soften any harshness that might result from a judgement in the law courts, on account of the firm principles they had to enforce. Later Equity developed a series of Maxims, as they were called, which embodied these milder and more humane principles, especially in land law. However a century ago there was a reform of our Court system. Part of this reform was deliberately to unite law and equity, as shown in the relevant section of the Act: 'In all matters . . . in which there is any conflict or variance between the Rules of Equity and the Rules of Common Law, with reference to the same matter, the Rules of Equity shall prevail.' (Supreme Court of Judicature Act 1873.)

Since then, though the word equity is often used, it is not, as is said, a technical term, or a term of art. It has its everyday meaning of fair dealing.

Judicial precedent

We have explained in the subsection on case law, how our law developed from the *ratio decidendi* involved in a case, whilst allowing also for the authority which that case possesses, due to the hierarchy of the Courts. Because these principles are so fundamental to our law, it may be helpful to observe judicial precedent at work, in two recent cases relating to areas of life of interest to the leisure services.

Beekeepers' Case (1985)[3]

The defendant sprayed his oilseed rape fields containing 23 acres with a pesticide, Hostathion. He did this mid-morning when bees were active, and known to be active, and many thousands died. Sued for damages he was found negligent. The case was said to break new legal ground, since it was about a crop sprayer's activities with his own property on his own land. However the Court dealt with it by applying the principle of *Donoghue v Stevenson* (*see* Chapter 4 Negligence – defences). This is briefly that if the person who knows others will be affected by his actions and whom he ought reasonably to have in mind as so affected, nonetheless acts without taking reasonable care for those persons and they are injured or suffer damage, then he is answerable for the consequences of his negligence.

In this case, the defendant knew the bees were present, namely on adjoining fields in abundance; he gave completely inadequate warning of his operation; he did not try to avoid harming the bees by the timing of his spraying operation; in short he was negligent.

Secondly, the Court considered whether the beekeepers might prudently have kept their bees away from the peril created by the spraying and so were partly negligent too. The options open to the beekeepers were, the experts said, either to close the hives altogether, when damage and deaths would have occurred or, alternatively, to have used the haycock method of shrouding their hives. Neither course would have been realistic said the Court, and so the plaintiffs won their case.

The Court found that the situation was one where the Donoghue principle could apply: they looked to see if the farmer showed reasonable care for the beekeepers and their hives: found that he did not do so: hence the farmer was liable for the resulting damage. It is a good example of old law being applied to new circumstances logically and firmly.

Go Kart Track Case (1986)[4]

Rochester Council let land to the Medway Kart Club which ran go kart races or practising sessions. This activity caused a serious nuisance to the three householders who lived directly opposite the track, on the other side of the River Medway. They presented formidable documented evidence to the Court of that nuisance, both in the scientific terms of the British Standard of decibel level and also in the personal terms of 'it was a noise like a chain saw or a bee inside a jar'. They said they couldn't hear the sound on their television sets. They called supporting evidence from neighbours.

The Court was pressed on the legal relation between the local authority and the occupying club and went back 100 years to find legal authority for a landowner being liable, when it was not he but his lessee who committed the nuisance. The case in question laid down the principle that, to incur liability, the owner had both to authorise the use and also to be aware that it might be expected to cause a nuisance. This was at the heart of the case brought against the Rochester Council and the Court referred to evidence given by the Recreation Officer of the Council and the other officers, who had reported to their authority on the implications of the go kart racing. Eventually the judge followed precedent and found for the plaintiffs.

He also looked at precedent when he considered the remedy he should grant to the plaintiffs. In the boat racing case of *Kennaway v Thompson*,[5] where a noise nuisance had to be controlled, the Court had evolved a careful balanced injunction – permitting so many international meetings, so many practice nights and specifying intervals of peace and quiet. Here, distinguishing his facts, the judge granted a complete injunction against any go kart racing on the site. The nuisance had been brought to the householders, he said. It was 'an offending operation'. Thus this case also provides an example of systematic application of legal precedents to a community problem, with logical and robust determination.

Classes of law

Criminal

It is tempting to define criminal law as that part of our total law which is enforced against a citizen by the Crown in the criminal courts, and which is likely to involve punishment if the case is made out. This will provide a simple contrast with civil law, in which one citizen is set against another citizen to enforce or dispute legal rights and duties affecting those two citizens.

In other words, having seen the difficulties that emerge when a definition is couched in theoretical terms, we centre ours on the Courts and the likelihood of punishment. This is also because we now have such a variety of crimes on our statute book that exceptions can easily be found to most definitions based on the crime itself. Table 1.2 seeks to highlight the nature of criminal law.

Table 1.2   Nature of criminal law

	Criminal	Civil
Form	State prosecutes citizen	Citizen sues another citizen
Purpose	Primarily punishment	Primarily putting right some wrong
Conclusion	Guilty or not guilty to be found by the Court	Satisfy the Court with the case brought
Nature of decision	Punishment, in varying forms	Payment of damages to the victor or secure an Order for Specific Performance or some other appropriate remedy

Act and intent

Having said that, we must emphasise that a crime involves an act such as stealing and an intent, namely to deprive the owner of that property permanently. This simple statement at once leads us to the nuances with which criminal law abounds. Was it an act or merely an attempt? Again, was the necessary intent present, perhaps driving recklessly or only carelessly? Was the accused sleepwalking or otherwise unaware of his acts? Did he act involuntarily, owing to threat or harm? And so on. Some statutes do provide that the necessary guilty intent shall be presumed unless the accused shows otherwise, eg being in possession of recently stolen goods, within the qualifications set out in the Theft Act 1968 section 27.

Groups of crimes

It may be helpful next to mention some of the main groups of crimes which are dealt with in the criminal law. These include those against public order, eg riot, or use of offensive weapons in public; or involving firearms; or those relating to the administration of justice, such as bribes, perjury or interfering with juries. Another group of crimes concern offences against property like blackmail, forgery, theft, criminal damage or burglary. The third group, concerning offences against people, covers murder, assault, rape and other graded forms of assault.

Another feature of criminal law is the classification it makes by reference to the method by which they are prosecuted. For instance, a very large proportion go on summons to be tried by magistrates. More serious crimes are called indictable, because the indictment is the name of the charge sheet used at the Crown Courts, where they are prosecuted. (It is incidentally at the Crown Courts that juries are used.) Then there is a middle group of offences which can be tried either summarily, ie before the magistrates, or on indictment.

Finally, we should mention that an offence which carries a possible punishment of five years imprisonment or more is called an arrestable offence. For this group a suspect can suffer arrest without warrant.

Civil

As indicated, civil law is the branch in which one citizen seeks to exercise legal rights against another. It embraces the wide range from trespass and nuisance to negligence, defamation and breach of contract. The law is sometimes contained in a statute and sometimes it is the common law. Unlike criminal law, where the sanction is the punishment of an offender, civil actions usually lead to damages ordered to be paid by the loser to the winner. The Courts also issue injunctions, to prevent repetition of unlawful conduct or prerogative orders in the case of public bodies – just another 'citizen' for this purpose – to correct some wrong they have caused, eg by mishandling an application for an entertainment licence. It is in civil law also that we meet the writ of *Habeas Corpus*, whereby a person, eg a prison governor, detaining another is ordered to bring him before the Court in order to see if the detention is justified or whether the Court should free the person in question. Lastly there is an order of the Court in civil law called Specific Performance. It can be used for example in a land dispute to compel a vendor to complete a sale from which, though legally committed, he has been trying to escape.

European law

Since 1972 this country has also been subject to the European law which is embodied in regulations or directives of the European Commission and Council of Ministers or else in decisions of the European Court of Justice at Luxemburg.

It was the European Communities Act 1972 which effected this important step. Since then Community law has been gradually filtering into our legal system. The topics it affects are limited by the Treaty of Rome of 1957 and subsequent treaties. They may be said to start with agriculture but they also cover commerce in many forms. Furthermore, personal rights have been publicised in recent cases. These can affect leisure service managers when they impinge on the rights of sportsmen to move freely between EEC countries. The contracts of musicians and others who pass between this country and the Continent may well come within Community law if breaches or other legal problems arise.

It may be helpful to try to summarise and illustrate the links which English law now has with Community law:

1 A Community Regulation has immediate force here, just like an Act of Parliament.

2 A Community Directive on the other hand requires member states to pass legislation of their own to achieve the standards it sets out. For instance this country has enacted several statutes in the fields of race and sex discrimination to comply with EC Directives. Similar response has also led to some of our recent company law.

3 Where there is conflict between Community law and UK law, Community law prevails.

4 In a recent case about amusement machines in public houses in the north of England, the Court had to conduct what the judge called 'a European safari' to ascertain the relevant law. *Cutsforth v Mansfield Inns Ltd* (1986)[6]

arose from a challenge by a firm in Humberside, which serviced these machines, to a move by the new owner of a chain of public houses to exclude them from the repairing and servicing work at these premises. The plaintiffs argued successfully that their proposed exclusion flouted Community law in restricting or distorting competition. The case had complexities which need not detain us here; at the stage reached, the Court granted an interim injunction to restrain the new owners from enforcing a new tied house agreement to exclude the plaintiffs from the business, at least until there was a full trial. In that setting the case is an interesting example of the direct application of Community law in the entertainment field.

THE PRACTICE

Courts, tribunals, arbitration

Courts

Figure 1.2 illustrates the Court system.

Figure 1.2 Court system

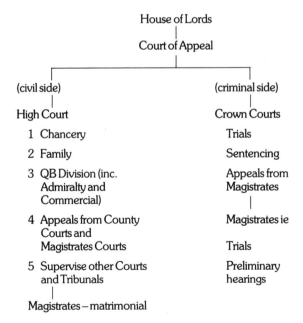

Magistrates Courts
Magistrates Courts are said to deal with more than 90 per cent of all Court cases. Presided over sometimes by a lawyer, a Stipendiary Magistrate, espe-

cially in large cities, they are more usually the scene of the lay magistrates after whom they are named. They usually sit in benches of three and are advised by a legally qualified clerk. Their cases are often motoring, on the criminal side, and matrimonial, on the civil side. They are limited to imposing a fine of £1000 or imprisonment for twelve months (if there are two charges).

Their cases sometimes lead to their deciding to send the offender to the Crown Court for a more severe sentence than they can impose. Certain offences offer the accused the choice to go to the Crown Court with its jury. In these and also the more serious crimes, where the Crown Court alone can try the case, the magistrates' function is to oversee the preliminary hearing, when one magistrate may sit alone. This committal proceeding, as it is called, consists of submitting the prosecution's evidence and if this is sufficient in the Court's view to make out what is called a *prima facie* case, then the Magistrates Court's role ends by committing the accused to the Crown Court for the full trial to take place there.

The Magistrates Courts do try cases under the Health and Safety at Work Act 1974, the Food Act 1984 and a wide variety of others in which leisure service managers may perforce become involved.

An appeal on a point of law goes to the Queen's Bench Divisional Court. An appeal against conviction or sentence goes to the Crown Court.

Crown Courts
These are the successors to the old Quarter Sessions and Assizes and deal with a great variety of serious cases, some initially, some for sentencing purposes as explained above and some in hearing appeals. In a busy city there can be as many as a dozen sitting at one time in the same building.

Queens Bench Divisional Court
This branch of the High Court hears appeals on points of law from Magistrates Courts. These are known as appeals by case stated.

County Courts
The County Court comes lowest in the civil court hierarchy. A judge adjudicates in cases where the sum involved is not more than £5000 and the law relates to tort and contract. He is assisted by another lawyer called the Registrar who tries some of the cases.

The High Court
This is the major Civil Court with the various divisions set out in the chart. One High Court judge sits on his own in the Queens Bench when handling cases receiving their first hearing. The Lord Chief Justice is the senior judge.

Court of Appeal
The Master of the Rolls presides here and sits with two other Lords Justices of Appeal. All its cases are on points of law.

House of Lords
The House of Lords is the supreme Court in this country. It may not handle

more than 100 cases in a year but its decisions are of the highest authority. Usually five Law Lords comprise the Court; the Lord Chancellor is in charge and sits himself from time to time.

Leapfrogging We should mention a procedure which in practice has not been greatly used whereby an appeal from the High Court can 'leapfrog' the Court of Appeal and go straight to the House of Lords in order to obtain a final decision. But both trial judge and the House of Lords have to agree that the issue justifies that course and so must the parties. It sounded a useful idea when enacted but it has not been popular.

Judicial Committee of the Privy Council The Law Lords who constitute the House of Lords also help to form what is called the Judicial Committee of the Privy Council. This has a considerable history and is still the highest Appeal Court in the Commonwealth. A Commonwealth judge will sit with the Court as constituted for this purpose; 25 countries are still making use of this appellate system.

Tribunals

There are numerous Tribunals at work in this country, each with a limited specialist jurisdiction. Usually they are presided over by a lawyer, sitting with specialist laymen. The ones perhaps encountered by leisure service managers will be Rent Tribunals about rent, Agricultural Land Tribunals about land disputes, especially tenancies, and Industrial Tribunals about employment law. These last ones were set up under the Employment Protection (Consolidation) Act 1978 and associated acts and deal with complaints about unfair dismissal, including redundancy. They are more informal than some we have been discussing. The Employment Appeal Tribunal handles appeals from Industrial Tribunals.

A Council on Tribunals has been set up to maintain oversight on the working of all these Tribunals.

Arbitration

Arbitration is an age old method of resolving disputes outside the Courts of Law. Building and other commercial contracts nowadays often provide for disputes arising under those arrangements to be settled by arbitration.

The pattern of arbitration will vary from contract to contract; the main aim will be to engage some specialists in the subject matter to form the arbitration panel, perhaps lawyers, structural engineers, architects, accountants or many others. The Advisory Conciliatory and Arbitration Service (ACAS) is the specialist arbitration service for employment disputes.

Arbitration is an informal procedure which allows the essence of the arguments on both sides to be put in written form. It is private yet still expensive and not always favoured. It is the nature of the dispute which determines whether it goes to the Courts or the arbitrator. An arbitrator's powers are strictly limited to the terms under which he is appointed; a Court, which can give damages, specific performance and injunctions, is usually more effective if the dispute is radical, deep and with far reaching consequences.

Even arbitrators can be subject to the Law Courts if it should emerge that the principles of natural justice were flouted.

Juries

Many citizens serve at least once in their lifetime on a jury. Citizens between 18 and 65 years old are eligible if they have lived in this country for five years since the age of 13.

Juries are now assembled by the Crown Courts where most trials needing their services take place. There are groups of persons who may be exempt from jury service, like lawyers who may know lawyers in the case or are otherwise handicapped from giving an impartial decision on the case to be tried.

It is the facts which the jury are regarded as best able to determine. Who do we believe? Did he drive that car or was his wife at the wheel? Was he wearing those shoes when those footprints were made near the haystack? Did the barman get him a skeleton key to the safe? And so on.

The judge, on the other hand, is responsible for the relevant law and the sentence, once the jury have reached a conclusion on the facts, which the judge sums up for them. They are still called and sworn as twelve but are not always to be unanimous if the judge decides, because of their difficulties, to take a majority verdict from ten of them.

Appeals system

It may be useful to summarise here what was necessarily intermingled with other discussion earlier about the general Court system.

1 The Queens Bench Divisional Court hears appeals from Magistrates Courts by case stated, ie summing up a critical point of law. The same Court hears appeals from some Tribunals.

2 The Court of Appeal (civil division) hears appeals from the High Court, the Employment Appeal Tribunal and Lands Tribunal and the County Courts, subject to certain qualifications. It does not take evidence from witnesses.

The Court of Appeal (criminal division) hears appeals from the Crown Courts.

3 The House of Lords hears appeals from the Court of Appeal. It also takes appeals from Scotland and Northern Ireland. The judgements are technically called 'speeches' since the Court is part of the House of Lords, as a branch of Parliament.

4 The Judicial Committee of the Privy Council hears appeals from Commonwealth countries, the Prize Court about Admiralty matters and one or two that do not concern us here.

The legal profession

It is convenient to deal with members as found today, rather than historically. Thus we shall describe briefly the status and role of judges, barristers, solicitors, legal executives and licensed conveyancers.

Judges

The majority of judges are barristers as described below. They have great experience of the legal system and the law and are highly regarded for their qualities. The Lord Chancellor is senior in the House of Lords, the Master of the Rolls in the Court of Appeal and the Lord Chief Justice in the High Court. Circuit judges preside in the Crown Courts. Some of the judges in Crown Courts are called recorders.

Solicitors can be judges in the Crown Courts. They, like barristers, must be of at least seven years' standing to be considered for such appointments.

Barristers

Barristers undergo their training by belonging to an Inn of Court, of which there are currently four in London. After passing two Bar examinations, sometimes linked to a law degree, they are 'called to the Bar' and their training continues while they serve twelve months as a pupil with a practising barrister.

They are primarily skilled advocates, with access to all the Courts. This is their speciality, whereas solicitors tend to be generalists. Within this skill, further specialities develop so that some barristers are known as belonging to commerce or tax or shipping chambers.

There are almost 5000 barristers in this country. They, like solicitors, are currently in the throes of professional practice reforms. As a profession, barristers have their own disciplinary procedures, via the Inns and the Bar Council. After experience as a barrister for some years, a person may be approved by the Lord Chancellor as a Queen's Counsel. This is a senior barrister who is normally accompanied in Court by a junior barrister and is also distinguishable by wearing a silk gown, rather than the ordinary stuff gown.

Solicitors

Solicitors now number over 40,000 in this country and, unlike barristers, who congregate in London and the large cities, they are to be found in every town in the land. They handle conveyancing of property, probate work with wills and intestacies, divorce, breach of contract and tort claims, employment and welfare law, to mention only the main topics. Some specialise in company law, shipping or commercial matters. Some are in the direct employment of local authorities, commercial companies or trades unions or become civil servants, in the employ of the Government. The number of partners in a firm of private solicitors can vary from one to thirty or more. The larger the firm, the more likely they are to specialise.

Their training is done via the Law Society and to become a qualified solicitor involves a period under Articles of two years if a law graduate and four-and-a-half years if not. The training contains both practical and academic elements and is tested at two stages of examinations. After admission to the Roll of solicitors, solicitors are nowadays subject to continued training to help to keep abreast of the changing law.

Solicitors can act as advocates in Magistrates Courts, County Courts, Coroners Courts and Tribunals. They engage or brief barristers to act as advocates in the higher Courts. It is indeed only after being so briefed that a barrister goes into Court.

Solicitors are 'commissioners for oaths' for the purpose of certifying affidavits which laymen desire to swear on all manner of subjects, for their use in legal proceedings.

Every solicitor contributes to a compensation fund, which is used to compensate clients who have suffered loss through some lack of professional expertise or attention by solicitors. In addition to this obligation, solicitors need a Practising Certificate, renewable annually, and can be disciplined and even struck off the Roll if found guilty by their professional tribunal of unprofessional conduct.

Legal executives

Legal executives are to be found in most solicitors' offices. They have to qualify by passing examinations of their own Institute in certain branches of the law and they are usually to be found working with solicitors in conveyancing, probate or litigation work. They form an invaluable part of the team which makes up a firm of solicitors. Their numbers have been given recently as more than 14,000. They are fulfilling the role formerly filled by persons called managing clerks.

Licensed conveyancers

The latest arrival on the legal scene is the licensed conveyancer. Small in numbers so far, these persons practise conveyancing only. They are under the discipline of a newly created Council, in respect of indemnity insurance, skill and standards. Historically, they stem from a decision in Parliament that a monopoly in conveyancing should not remain with solicitors. Ironically, some solicitors have taken out this licence, as conveyancing specialists only.

Day to day litigation

We describe now the course of criminal and then civil actions in our Courts.

Criminal case

This begins with a summons obtained before a magistrate by the police or a citizen and served on the defendant. Alternatively, in many and certainly all the serious offences, a person is charged with an offence, the charge being then reduced to writing. In both ways, the accused knows the case he has to meet. If the case is for trial in the Crown Court, the charge is contained in a document called an indictment.

In Court, whether Magistrates or Crown, the prosecution present their case by an address to the Court, support it with evidence from witnesses and allow those witnesses to be cross examined by the other side and questioned by the Court. The defence follow the same procedure and there follow final addresses from each side, summarising their hopes for the decision, in the light of the evidence. In the Magistrates Court, the Bench then retire and come back with their decision. In the Crown Court, the jury is then addressed by the judge, who summarises the evidence and the issues on which their decision is sought, to enable them to answer the traditional 'guilty or not guilty?' on their return from confidential deliberation.

Civil case

The chief difference to the observer is the emphasis on documents. In the High Court, it is the writ and particulars of claim which start most proceedings. The latter can be lengthy and the language complex. The defendant's lawyers put in a defence, replying to the points made. There is then a stage called interlocutory, for further particulars to be established by both parties, documents to be 'discovered' ie revealed, whether letters, photographs perhaps of the location, the chipped swimming pool surround or the faulty strut in the sports centre, or possibly experts' reports.

The aim is to limit the time in Court to arguments about the essential issues between the parties. Each side will usually admit, ie agree, some of the facts but wish to argue the main issue, for example negligence, contributory negligence, in tort or lack of misrepresentation, maybe in breach of contract disputes.

The Court scene resembles the one described above, with the plaintiff's advocate first addressing the Court, calling witnesses, subjecting them to cross examination and then the defendant following the same sequence with his case and witnesses.

In this civil case, where juries are rarely found, though notoriously still used in defamation cases, the judge then gives his judgement, unless he reserves it a little while before reaching his final decision. The victor's legal costs will normally have to be paid by the loser; these can be agreed between the parties or settled by a Court officer.

The niceties and complexities of litigation are many but the bare outline offered here should indicate at least the framework into which other details can be fitted.

Limitation of actions at law

It is important for leisure service managers to know that there are time limits imposed by our law on bringing cases in the Courts, both civil and criminal.

On the one hand it is proper that citizens should be able to establish their rights in Court; on the other, it is equitable that persons should know when their worries are over and that litigation about a particular dispute cannot take place.

Criminal

So, on the criminal side, a case before magistrates must normally be commenced by summons taken out within six months of an offence, eg for false weights or measures or impure food sold at the football stadium cafeteria.

Civil

There is a Limitation Act which contains the time limits for various classes of civil cases to be commenced. This endeavours to hold the balance between the various considerations set out above. For instance, three years from the time 'when the cause of action arose' is stipulated for personal accident cases, whilst twelve years is allowed in another class of case about mistakes or fraud in documents. Lawyers have to take account of these limits and can be held to account if they fail to meet them in launching cases for clients. Laymen cannot be expected to know about them in any detail.

Yet they are a vital element in our legal system. The current tendency is to soften the penalising effect of these provisions. For instance, under the Employment Acts, a person dismissed from his job has three months in which to complain to an industrial tribunal for unfair dismissal. However that time can be extended if it is found that the person could not reasonably have presented his application within that three month period.

Again, in civil actions for damages, a recent distinction has become important between cases where there are personal injuries suffered and those where there are not. The Latent Damage Act 1986 extends this importance and introduces the new concept of a 'long stop' date when making these calculations. Starting from the cause of action, fifteen years is the long stop date, after which an action is out of legal time. Other refinements cannot be pursued here.

Notes

1 *Gething v Lynn* (1831) 109 ER 1130.
2 *New Windsor Corporation v Mellor* (1975) 3 AER 44.
3 *Tutton v A. D. Walter Ltd* (1985) 3 AER 757.
4 *Tetley v Chitty* (1986) 1 AER 663.
5 *Kennaway v Thompson* (1980) 3 AER 329.
6 *Cutsforth v Mansfield Inns Ltd* (1986) 1 AER 577.

The author takes this opportunity to disclaim any intentional sexual discrimination in this book. Where the text uses male terms please take as read the addition 'or the feminine equivalent' and, of course, vice versa for female references.

2 Statutory powers of local authorities

Public Health Acts

There are five Public Health Acts on our Statute Book which are relevant to leisure service managers. In addition to those successive Statutes of 1875, 1890, 1907, 1925 and 1961, the Local Government (Miscellaneous Powers) Act of 1976 contains its quota of related provisions. It will doubtless seem strange to find the local authority powers to manage parks, boats, fairs and swimming pools in Acts with such titles. The time may indeed come when we have one Leisure Services Act, which consolidates 30 to 40 separate sections from the above Acts. At present we work with a well used Parliamentary practice of placing local government powers in Local Government Acts, after nearly a century of using Public Health Acts also as the vehicle for that class of law. We accordingly turn to describe those powers, grouped here according to subject.

Parks and recreation grounds

Provision of facilities
The initial power in the Public Health Act 1875 is to provide and manage 'public walks or pleasure grounds'. From the Victorian contentment with a public variant of the stately home's lawns, terraces, promenades and laid out gardens, Parliament has sanctioned wider and wider extensions of use. These now include hiring of pleasure boats (Act of 1890 section 44), skating, games and refreshment rooms (Act of 1907 sections 76 and 77), the right to charge when the park is used for football, cricket and other games (Act of 1925 section 56), power to enclose parts of the park for concert halls (Local Government Act 1972 section 145) and erection of ancillary buildings, including a caretaker's bungalow.

It must be noted that Parliament has safeguarded public rights by forbidding councils from letting more than one third of a park for exclusive use, or letting more than a quarter of all its public parks in that manner (Act of 1961 section 52). Similarly, if refreshment rooms or reading rooms are let to clubs, there is a maximum of twelve days per annum to be observed and another of four consecutive days. However more recently in the Local Government Act 1972 section 145, local authorities have been given power to set apart part of a park for use for dancing or entertainment without those proportional restraints. These uses include a concert hall, band or orchestral concerts, premises for dancing and exhibitions of arts and crafts.

Closures

Ordinary powers of management include legal limits on the power to close a public park eg for an agricultural show. Closure is permitted on only twelve days in a year and only six of these can be consecutive (Act of 1890 section 44, Act of 1961 section 53).

Byelaws

Another important power in relation to public parks is the power to make byelaws (Public Health Act 1875 section 164). These will usually cover for example noise from radio controlled aircraft, disorder, litter, cycling, bonfires and picnics, among other matters. Perhaps these would also cover facilities like a trim track, as well as a subject like use by dogs.[1]

Though the power to make the byelaws is statutory, it is the common law which has developed the way byelaws can be lawfully employed. It was a leading case, *Kruse v Johnson*,[2] in Kent in the 1890s, which was the pace setter. It concerned a byelaw forbidding music within 50 yards of a dwellinghouse. This was tested in the Courts and the High Court formulated four tests of the validity of a byelaw. These are that it must be certain, meaning lucid, it must be consistent with the general law, it must be within the powers of the byelaw making authority and, lastly, and perhaps most difficult, it must be reasonable.

It was this last test which was at the heart of the case of *Burnley B. C. v England*[3] in 1979 about dogs in parks. The local authority won, since the Courts approved their cautious approach to a banning byelaw. Wishing to place limits on dogs in their parks, they limited scheduled exclusions to 141 acres out of 795 acres in their borough. Furthermore, in their selection of areas to be kept free of dogs, they placed emphasis on children's play areas, ornamental gardens and playgrounds. This led the Court to say that the byelaw was not 'a gratuitous interference with the rights of others'.

It is another significant point in relation to byelaws that the mere act of making them has been regarded in the Courts as extending the legal presence of the local authority in the park affected. The authority may be liable if they allow a nuisance which can be prevented by the use of byelaws. This is because their duty is to provide the park and then it is the public who enjoy and must be allowed to use it. This principle comes from the leading case of *Hall v Beckenham Corporation*[4] in 1949, which related to the control of the noise created by model aircraft.

The appropriation of a public park to another use or even its disposal is now legally possible, provided that the statutory requirements can be met (Local Government and Land Act 1980 sections 122 and 123).

Sports centres and other major leisure facilities

Without doubt, the major empowering provision in this field is now section 19 of the Local Government (Miscellaneous Provisions) Act 1976, which we set out:

1 A local authority may provide, inside or outside its area, such recreational facilities as it thinks fit and, without prejudice to the generality of the powers conferred . . . those powers include in particular powers to provide:

    a   indoor facilities consisting of sports centres, swimming pools, skating rinks, tennis, squash and badminton courts, bowling centres, dance studios and riding schools;

    b   outdoor facilities consisting of pitches for team games, athletics grounds, swimming pools, tennis courts, cycle tracks, golf courses, bowling greens, riding schools, camp sites, and facilities for gliding;

    c   facilities for boating and water skiing on inland and coastal waters and for fishing;

    d   premises for the use of clubs or societies having athletic social or recreational objects;

    e   staff, including instructors, in connection with any such facilities or premises;

    f   such facilities in connection with any other recreational facilities as the authority considers it appropriate to provide, including . . . facilities by way of parking spaces and places at which food drink and tobacco may be bought from the authority or from another . . . person . . . and it is hereby declared that the(se) powers . . . include powers to provide buildings, equipment, supplies and assistance of any kind.

The section goes on to confer powers for local authorities to provide these facilities free or for payment. It allows grants or loans by a local authority towards the expenses of a voluntary organisation which is providing any of these section 19 facilities. (Voluntary organisation is defined as a person carrying on an undertaking 'otherwise than for profit'.)

Miscellaneous

Fairgrounds
A local authority has power to make byelaws for fairgrounds. These will doubtless deal with order, cleanliness, outbreaks of fire and public safety but they are not restricted to these topics (Act of 1961 section 75; Act of 1976 section 22).

Building regulations and theatres
The Building Act 1984 is the present parent Statute for building regulations, under which, along with a multitude of other subjects, theatres can be controlled in respect of their exits and entrances – the buildings, that is, not the actors. Enforcement of such regulations may well fall to an architect or engineer of the authority rather than a leisure service manager; the latter may however need to know of this control if he should find himself required to manage a civic theatre.

Swimming
There is a byelaw making power in the Public Health Act 1936 section 223 about swimming pools. Such byelaws can be a useful legal support for pool attendants in relation to disorderly conduct and ultimately exclusion of persons persisting in unsocial behaviour.

There is also power to make byelaws about swimming at the seaside (section 231). These may well deal with bathing huts, life saving appliances, and the management of pleasure boats in relation to safe bathing areas.

Licensing of pleasure boats
It is the Public Health Acts Amendment Act 1907 which contains the legal code for the licensing of pleasure boats and their owners (section 94).

a It is both the boats and the boatmen who are licensed. Licences can be revoked or suspended when the public interest so demands. The license holder can appeal against such action.
b It is an offence to let a boat unless licensed.
c The section operates only when an Order of the Home Secretary is in force in the area in question.
d A local authority can make byelaws to regulate the use of pleasure boats, especially in relation to safety and noise (Local Government Planning and Land Act 1980 section 185).
e The boatman's licence is annual and a fee is payable (Act of 1976 section 18). This licence is unnecessary if a licence from the Department of Trade and Industry is held for the boat in question.

Open Space Act 1906

This Act has survived as a useful code of law for two purposes: managing unfenced public playing and walking areas and, secondly, managing public cemeteries. Leisure service managers will be chiefly interested in the powers in the Act for managing such land, making byelaws and perhaps putting such land to other though related use.

Management

The Act contains an elaborate treatment of ways in which land could be acquired by a local authority for open space use. These tell of a different age and were designed to help trustees of charities, owners of land surrounded by houses or land held under statutory trusts, to transfer such land lawfully into public ownership.

Once acquired, the land comes under a broad duty imposed on the local authority in section 10 of the Act of 1906. It is to be kept in a decent state; it can have money spent on it to level or drain it, light it and fence it, provide seats, plants, ornaments – doubtless with a different meaning nowadays – and carry out improvements. Lastly, all this is to be within the general duty of holding it in trust to allow the public to enjoy it as an open space and for no other purpose.

By the Local Government Act 1988, Part 1, compulsory competitive tendering has been introduced for certain services of local authorities and these include ground maintenance and vehicle maintenance. The scheme is to oblige an authority to obtain three realistic tenders which can be considered along with the price from the authority's own works department. Current government plans will add to these services the management of sporting and leisure services. The list given is: sports centres, leisure centres, swimming pools, leisure pools, golf courses, putting greens, bowling greens, tennis courts, athletic tracks, pitches for team and other games, cycle tracks, water sports and leisure facilities, ski slopes, skating rinks and indoor bowling facilities.

It would also include supervising activities such as lifeguards at swimming pools, providing instruction, catering, provision and hire of sports equipment, employment and relevant training of staff.

The date by which such competitive tendering is planned is the beginning of 1993, although some would be twelve months sooner. The full implications and form of this major change are still to be settled as we go to print.

The Act goes into considerable detail about the way in which competing tenders are obtained. The spirit and indeed the letter of this new, important, law is perhaps best shown by section 7(7). This makes it a condition that a local authority does not, before reaching a decision to do the work in question, 'act in a manner having the effect . . . of restricting, distorting or preventing, competition'. Details in Part 1 relate to keeping accounts, preparing annual reports on these activities and giving information about the prices in the other tenders, if the authority decides to use its own staff for the work. Further, the minister can set targets for the listed work, on the basis of rates of return on capital. It should be noted that at a late stage in the Parliamentary debates, a section was added to this Act which outlaws the use of a local authority created company to do the work in question (section 33). The implications of this 'challenge of change' as it has been called, are far-reaching but clearly include:

1 the need to compete with private sector companies tailor made for competition;
2 the production of separate accounts for each defined activity including an allocation of the full cost of support services, and,
3 since fixed prices will be the norm, the delivery of services on time and on target;
4 making an acceptable return on capital investment.

These are momentous changes and the outcome will be awaited with the keenest interest.

Byelaws

An enduring problem for a local authority is to hold the balance between the interests of the different groups in their locality in the uses encouraged on say the Stray at Harrogate, the grassed areas laying behind the promenade at many seaside resorts and countless other open spaces lying in the middle of housing estates or elsewhere. It is here that byelaws play their part. By section 15 of this Act of 1906, authorities may make byelaws to regulate the use, ensure maintenance of order, and prevent nuisances and, finally, control admission and remove offenders.

In so far as these powers correspond to those used in public parks, some authorities use a common set of byelaws for both classes of territory.

It has become common practice since the last war to convert disused burial grounds into lawn cemeteries. This can take place usually when the burial ground is full and a detailed procedure of public notice and liaison with the Home Office must be followed. Nevertheless the practice comes within this Act and at the end of the exercise there can be a pleasant sitting out or promenade area, often in the midst of housing. Byelaws as above can be made for such lawn cemeteries.

Other uses

Land pressures in recent years have led to legislation which permits a local authority to convert open space land to other use. It is the Local Government Planning and Land Act 1972 which deals with this practice. Hence, where land is held under the Act of 1906 section 10 and is no longer required for these purposes (a matter for the authority, acting in good faith), then the land may be appropriated to another use. This action will not eliminate third party interests in the land; these will have to be negotiated away separately. An example might be a right of light lawfully acquired by a house which overlooks the open space.

Again, the above Act of 1980 permits the disposal of open space land but only with the consent of the Secretary of State.[5] The disposal exercise is protected by a number of conditions. The proposal has to be advertised and objections considered. Receipts from the sale have to be dealt with under directions under the Charities Act 1960. The act of disposal does not remove third party rights, as in the case above; that must be done as a separate exercise. Finally, disposal of open space land is in its nature such a major step, since the land was acquired under a public trust to keep it as open space for the public, that the Courts can still be called upon by the judicial review procedure initiated by an aggrieved party, to examine if the authority has departed from the legal obligations laid upon them. Likewise the Audit Commission may check on the merits and finances of such a transaction.

Commons Acts

This is another area of our law which awaits consolidation. It is contained in statutes which extend from 1876 to 1965. Here we shall describe the law as it affects the nature and management of a common and, secondly, ways of putting a common to alternative use.

Legal nature of a common

In early days inhabitants of a village had rights over the common land of that village. These included taking turf, grazing animals, taking timber and taking acorns for their pigs. Their rights were limited: they were in law the commoners' right of usage. The ownership of the land would rest in the lord of the manor.

As time went by, and the population increased, common land went out of fashion. Agriculture encouraged separate farms, rotation of crops encouraged separate ownership and cultivation. The era of Inclosure Acts came to its climax in the eighteenth and nineteenth centuries when no less than 4000 such Acts were passed. By each of these, land was taken out of a common and allocated to individuals or perhaps to special community use, like new highways. At length, tiring of this burden upon its time, Parliament approved a code of clauses which could be applied to the process of 'enclosing' a common. This was in 1845 and it greatly simplified the procedure.

Later, in 1876, Parliament stipulated that the enclosure of common land must take account of community interests such as recreation, amenity, trees and highways of all kinds. This was a major reform. In 1899 another Commons Act allowed a local authority to make a Scheme of Management for a common for which it was responsible. This is still done nowadays. Such a scheme has to take account of everything involved in good estate management, from drains and fences to parking places, seats and the preservation of historical objects or features. It is indeed a very comprehensive document.

Lastly, in this historical survey, in 1965 Parliament set in train a procedure to register existing common land. The Act, called the Commons Registration Act, requires registration of land, including village greens, and also the rights over the land. At the end of prescribed periods, no common land or rights of common had legal validity unless registered. Legal registers were established, to be kept by the registration authority under the Act, and the process of registration was linked with the Land Registration Acts, which go back to 1925. Those Acts deal with the registration of legal rights of all sorts, eg options to purchase land.

The Act of 1965 included a procedure for resolving objections to applications for registration; reports of hearings to settle these disputes can be studied.[6] Local authorities have a key role in this process, as land can be vested in them if it should happen that no other owner is known, as may well occur with a village green.

The New Forest, Epping Forest and the Forest of Dean are exempted from this Act. The minister can exempt other areas.

It will be evident that, over a lengthy period, we have reached a stage where the information about the legal existence of a common can be ascertained without undue difficulty. It may be that the desire to protect commons or open spaces leads a local authority into a need to confer with the Countryside Commission, as to which *see* Chapter 8.

Putting common land to commercial use

The special feature of commons is the interests of three parties, viz the owners, the commoners and the community. Thus the decision to put common land to another use is one that necessarily involves publicity and concurrence by a number of persons. Under the Town and Country Planning Act

1971, the consent of the Secretary of State for the Environment is also needed (section 123). This is available when a local authority hold the land for 'planning purposes', as the Act describes land acquired or appropriated under Part V of that Act (section 112). The local authority may, with the Secretary of State's consent, appropriate that land to a purpose, eg housing or highways, which is necessary at that time, or dispose of the land to someone else. In each instance the requirements of good planning have to be met. The best consideration has to be obtained in the case of a disposal (section 123(8)).

Caravans, buildings and refreshments
In two other statutes commons have been protected against being used for purposes outside those intended by their nature. In the Caravan Sites and Control of Development Act 1960, local authorities can make orders to regulate caravan sites; these may deal with caravans on a common and prohibit such use. In the second Act, the Countryside Act 1968, accommodation and refreshments for persons resorting to common land may be provided by local authorities, though only if the existing facilities are inadequate (section 9).

Allotments

Local authorities are allotment authorities. This means that they must provide land for allotments, where there is a demand. Whilst the councils make the final judgement about the strength of that demand, the law is that a representation by six or more electors in a locality for allotments to be provided is to be recognised as one calling for formal consideration (Allotment Act 1908 section 23).

The allotment authorities may be the district councils, London boroughs, parish councils in England or community councils in Wales. When a parish council elects to exercise such powers under the Allotment Acts, the district council for that area does not do so. Major powers are to be found in the Small Holdings and Allotments Act 1908, the Allotments Act 1922 and the Allotments Act 1950.

The main legal provisions which affect the management of allotments by local authorities concern tenure, rent and termination of tenancies.

Tenure

The tenancy of an allotment is yearly, in the sense that the normal notice of termination must be twelve months. Allotments must not be sublet, without the landlord's consent. The tenancy agreement cannot restrict the keeping of hens or rabbits (Act of 1950 section 12). The letting can be to an association or to persons on a cooperative basis, provided that the division of profits among members is controlled (Act of 1908 section 27). Local authorities have power to make rules setting out the general terms to be applied in regulating allotments in their area (Act of 1908 section 28).

Rent

The rent must be 'such as a tenant may reasonably be expected to pay for the land, taking into account the proposed terms' (Act of 1950 section 10). With little guidance available on the interpretation of this expression, a court in 1980 upheld a claim by an allotment tenant that his rent was unreasonable. From 90p in one year and £3 in the next, it had jumped to £10 in the third year. The decision, in the case of *Harwood v Borough of Reigate and Banstead* (1980)[7] was based on the view that it was expected that the cost of providing allotments by local authorities would be subsidised, as happens with other public leisure services. The court said that the rent increases should be in line with increases in charges for other recreational activities. Moreover, it was to be one appropriate to a notional, not an actual, tenant.

Termination

The normal twelve months notice to terminate an allotment tenancy must expire between 29 September and 6 April ie 'the close season' (Act of 1922 section 1). Three month notices are exceptionally permitted if:

  a The tenancy agreement stipulates that the land might be needed for roads, sewers, building, mining, industrial or housing use and that situation has arisen, or
  b the land is held by the landlord for a non-agricultural use and the land is needed for that use, which was set out in the tenancy agreement (Act of 1922 section 1).

Re-entry is also permitted for breach of covenant or non-payment of rent (ibid). Termination gives rise to a liability on the landlord to compensate the tenant for his growing crops and fertilisers and also paying him a sum equal to one year's rent, in respect of disturbance to his tenancy. A tenant has the right to remove huts, greenhouses, fruit trees and bushes. If on the other hand, the landlord can show a lack of good cultivation by the tenant, he can counter-claim a sum against these payments which the law requires him to make.

Conclusion

Allotment gardening is popular with about half a million people in our country. It is rooted in history, when land was allotted or allocated for recreational gardening under the Poor Law or the Enclosure Acts. It is an important part of modern leisure services.

Protection of trees

The law about trees is almost worth a small book on its own. It would have to deal with the Forestry Commission, the Common Law about nuisances caused by branches or the roots of trees and the legislation about Dutch Elm disease, to name only a few items.

Here we look at the area of law which relates to Tree Preservation Orders. These would seem to be a critical feature in the preservation of our countryside, when we are considering the powers of local authorities.

The Town and Country Planning Act 1971 (section 59) expressly requires a local authority to ensure that adequate provision is made for preserving or planting trees, when they are handling every application for planning permission for development.

Secondly, those authorities are placed under a duty to make such Tree Preservation Orders as appear to be necessary in connection with the granting of planning permission.

These wide duties have to be seen in the context of the duties we have described later for local authorities, among others, to conserve the natural beauty and amenity of the countryside (Countryside Act 1968 section 11). We now summarise the basic features of this law:

1 It relates to a single tree, a group or a woodland and must be made in the interests of the amenities of the area.

2 It must not conflict with activity of the Forestry Commission nor relate to Crown land, subject to certain exceptions.

3 There is power to enter land to survey it for the purposes of a Tree Preservation Order.

4 The procedure is for the planning authority to make the Order, serve it on the owners and occupiers and then allow an objection period before deciding, as an authority, whether to 'confirm' the Order.

5 The Order is registered as a Local Land Change, so that purchasers of the land may learn about it. The Act is supported by regulations which embody the detail that is necessary about this procedure. Occasionally, one of these Orders is needed in a hurry.

6 The complementary provision is then to create offences for damage or felling a tree which is within a Tree Preservation Order. There are exceptions for the case of good husbandry, for the case of the authority's own trees and also one for trees of less than a specified diameter.

7 A defence is created for the owner who serves six weeks notice of intention to, perhaps, lop or top an identified tree and who then carries out his intent, either with the consent of the local planning authority or, in the absence of that consent, is able to show that the authority were aware of his intention – on the basis of the adage that silence signifies assent.

8 An obligation to replace a tree removed, uprooted or destroyed in contravention of this code of law is also included in the Act of 1971 (section 62).

Caravans

Licensing of caravan sites was introduced in 1960 in the Caravan Sites and Control of Development Act of that year. The pattern of legal control now developed after many cases and a wealth of experience in National Parks and elsewhere, is summarised below:

1 The grant of a site licence accompanies planning permission for that use (Act of 1960 section 3). If the planning permission has a time limit on it, then the Caravan Site Licence expires at the same time.

2 The local authority issues the licence.

3 The licence is primarily about internal management of the site, ie numbers, amenities, types, location, fire fighting, sanitary arrangements. Cases have shown which conditions in such a licence go too far, eg in fixing rents, as in

Mixnam's Properties v Chertsey U.D.C. (1965)[8] and, on the other hand, what is acceptable in law, eg *Esdell Caravan Parks Ltd v Hemel Hempstead U.D.C.* (1965),[9] where the effect of a large number of caravan dwellers on the educational, transport and shopping provision in a locality was allowed to be taken into account, in reducing from 78 to 24 the permitted number of caravans in a licence.

4 A right of appeal against conditions is available; it goes to the Magistrates Court, where the main test of a valid condition is whether it is 'unduly burdensome'.

5 The local authority can inspect the site, on giving 24 hours' notice.

6 Breaches of conditions in a licence can lead to prosecution. A third conviction can lead to revocation of the licence.

7 Twelve exceptions have been created to this need for a Site Licence of which examples are: forestry workers, exempted organisations (eg Boy Scouts organisation, Caravan Club; these have a maximum of five days), building sites, fairground people and gypsies on a municipal site.

Town and country planning

The legal powers of local authorities have developed over the last 150 years from small beginnings with public parks, museums and libraries. Town planning was a comparatively late arrival in the portfolio of powers available at town and county halls, compared with public health and housing. However since 1945, in particular, redevelopment and reconstruction of urban centres and control of the balance of land available for urban and rural use have led local planning authorities to be given more and more powers by Parliament. We consider here the basic features of the present system.

Local planning authorities

In the six metropolitan areas and London, there is one local planning authority, namely the district council or London borough council, as the case may be. In the rest of the country, it is the county council which is the planning authority for the county and the district council is the planning authority for the district. The exception is land falling within National Parks, which comes within the control of a joint or special planning board for that Park, if there is such an authority constituted for that National Park (Town and Country Planning Act 1971 section 1, Local Government Acts 1972 and 1985) ie the Lake District Special Planning Board and the Peak District Planning Board.

In practice, some of the powers of local planning authorities are delegated to committees, sub-committees and officers, in order to encourage the efficient flow of town planning applications and other town planning business.

Applications, consents and powers of control

The basic town planning control under the Town and Country Planning Acts is related to 'development'. A person wishing to carry out 'development' must seek planning permission by means of a planning application (Act of 1971 section 25).

'Development'

'Development' is defined as being 'the carrying out of building, engineering, mining or other operations in, on, over, or under land or the making of any material change in the use of any buildings or other land' (Act of 1971 section 22).

Each part of this definition has given rise to numerous tests of its application to particular situations, since used in the Town and Country Planning Act 1947. The current Act of 1971 itself clears the ground by eliminating from development control, as it is called, many forms of routine building and engineering works. These include road works, repair and renewal of public utilities under roads, the routine maintenance of buildings, the use of land within the curtelage of a dwellinghouse for 'purposes incidental to the enjoyment of the dwellinghouse as such' (Act of 1971 section 22).

These excluded activities include the very important ones of agriculture and forestry. The exclusions also refer to a sophisticated part of town planning law known as the Use Classes. This feature allows a change in the use from, say, a sportswear shop to a children's wear shop without the need for planning permission; this is because the present and the future use will be in the same Use Class. The law is that when the change of use involves moving from one listed Use Class to another planning permission is needed. The present Use Classes Order, dating from 1987, has sixteen such classes. It also leaves outside its framework seven specified uses, which must therefore be dealt with by ordinary control. These include a theatre, an amusement arcade or centre and a funfair.

The last point to note on this topic is that it is only a *material* change of use which requires planning permission. Naturally this word has given rise to much argument. We are given two special examples in the Act itself, namely the making of two or more separate dwellings out of one, and secondly, the deposit of refuse on land, even if already used for that purpose, if the effect is to extend the surface area or to increase the height so that it is higher than the surrounding land.

A number of refinements have grown up over the years from decisions of the Courts or the Secretary of State. It is not easy to find many affecting leisure services, apart perhaps from caravan parks. It is of interest that to change the intensity of such use from, say, eight caravans to 80 may still, whilst clearly caravan use, be looked on as so changing the character of the site as to be a *material* change of use and, therefore, requiring planning permission.

'Calling them in'

Some applications, apparently straightforward, give rise to objections when advertised, so that even the initial hearing of the application becomes a debate. However, at the level of officer, sub-committee, committee or council, a decision will be given. The exception is if the application for planning permission is for, say, a new shopping centre, and thus so substantial in its implications that the Secretary of State decides to determine it – 'call it in', as it is said. He has to be informed by the local planning authority when an application will involve a departure from the area, local or structure plan, where the planning policies for the areas of district and county are set out.

Outline applications
Some developments are such that it is prudent to ascertain the views of the local planning authority about the principle of the change of use or building, as the case may be, before devoting a lot of expense to working up detailed plans. This situation has given rise to what are called outline applications, followed by detailed applications; whilst these are a small proportion, they are a settled, useful and vital part of the whole process.

Each local planning authority keeps a register of approved planning permissions. It is one of the items a purchaser of property will be interested in inspecting, before be completes his purchase.

The subject easily becomes complex and we have endeavoured to describe the basic features only. It should be noted, however, that among the other specialist aspects are the controls over trees by Tree Preservation Orders, as described earlier in this chapter, and also advertisements and listed (meaning protected) buildings of historical or architectural interest. These last are in various categories of eminence, and run the gamut from the Tower of London to the humblest market cross.

Appeals

There is a right of appeal to the Secretary of State when an application for planning permission has been refused. A similar right is exercisable against a condition in an approved planning permission to which exception is taken by the applicant. A right is also given if the local planning authority has not given its decision on an application within eight weeks of receipt (or an agreed extension) (Act of 1971 section 36). The appeal can be dealt with at an enquiry conducted by an inspector appointed by the Secretary of State. If the Secretary of State so decides, he may indeed leave the inspector to determine the appeal himself.

Enquiries are held currently in about 15 per cent of appeals, the balance being determined, by agreement of the parties, on documentary submissions.

A decision on an appeal is final, unless a party decides that a point of law is involved and goes to the Courts to resolve it.

Building regulations

Building regulations are the legal control over the standards for materials and methods of construction used in buildings. They are made by the Secretary of State for the Environment but enforced by local authorities and the present regulations are the successors of similar ones used in this country for many years. They are regularly altered in order to keep pace with the tremendous changes in materials and practices in recent years. An application for building regulation consent must be made before building work starts. Like planning permissions in this respect, building regulation consents are imperative: work begun without them can be penalised to the ultimate extent of being ordered to be pulled down.

A fee is payable on submission of an application, as with planning permissions.

With some types of building, eg a house, the opportunity for a Building Inspector to see the various stages as it progresses is a legal requirement, eg the drains and the damp course. But an initial notice has to be given by all builders to alert the authority before work starts and the authority will settle the visits and stages of work that need approval, according to the particular building work.

The present regulations are made under the Building Act 1984, a comprehensive statute on this whole subject.

Just as we said that applicants for planning permission were ready to argue the question of *material* change of use, so builders are ready to seek the relaxation of the building regulations for particular schemes and materials, eg about the thickness of glass in a particular location or plastic instead of a different type of piping in another (Building Act 1984 section 8). It is this sort of question that can give rise to appeals against refusals to relax (section 39). There is indeed in that Act of 1984 a system of submissions, decision, appeals and enforcement.

Part II of the Building Act deals with the right of a developer to opt for a building inspector other than a local authority employee to supervise his work. The liaison needed when his option is taken is spelt out in the Act and Regulations.[10]

Water recreation

We consider here the forms of water recreation that local authorities provide or manage, viz boating, National Parks and the seaside. Other popular water leisure pursuits include fishing, for which the complex licensing and enforcement legislation falls to be administered by the Water Authorities; canals for pleasure purposes, where the British Waterways Board is the managing authority; and inland waters, such as reservoirs, when Water Authorities are again the responsible legal managers. Harbour authorities and navigation authorities have their own areas of responsibility on the coast under the Water Resources Acts of 1963 and 1973.

Water and the Common Law

Firstly however, it may be convenient to summarise the principles developed in our Common Law about water.

1 Water can only be 'owned' when collected within say, a pool, tank or reservoir. When flowing, it is not able to be owned.

2 The bed of non-tidal rivers and streams however does belong to the adjoining owners. If there is no contrary evidence on the title deeds, then the law is that these riparian owners, as they are called, each own to the centre line of the watercourse in question. If the same person should happen to be the

owner of the land on both sides of the river or stream, then he would own the whole river or stream bed.

3 Water can be taken from such a stream for domestic or agricultural purposes but a Water Authority licence is needed for abstraction of water for business purposes (Water Resources Act 1973 section 24).

4 The riparian owners enjoy, and so can legally grant to others, the right of navigation in the watercourse adjacent to their land holding. But without a specific grant, such a right will not extend to landing, mooring, fishing or towing along that part of the bank.

Boats

'Facilities for boating' can be provided by a local authority under the Local Government (Miscellaneous Provisions) Act 1976 (section 19) and this covers a jetty or landing stage or associated buildings.

If such boats are to be used to carry passengers for hire, the local authority will license them, under the Public Health Acts (Amendment) Act 1907. The licences will detail such matters as the name of the licensee being displayed on the boat, and the permitted number of passengers. A fee will be charged for the licence. There is power to suspend or revoke such a licence, in the public interest (ibid section 94).

The boatmen themselves need a separate licence (*see* Act of 1907 section 94 and Local Government (Miscellaneous Provisions) Act 1976 section 18).

Byelaws can be made, if the local usage justifies that step and these will doubtless deal with matters such as silencers, the carrying capacity, the range of activity, use in order to avoid inconvenience to other persons and general good practice. Such byelaws are effective within 1000 yards of the shore; they must not conflict with byelaws of authorities manning docks or piers in the locality.

National Parks

We describe later the intimate involvement of local authorities in some aspects of the management of these Parks; it is quite possible that boating, fishing and bathing will take place in such areas. Local authorities have powers to provide facilities for these leisure services, under the National Parks and Access to the Countryside Act 1949 (section 13) and the Countryside Act 1968 (sections 12–13). These Acts contain the important condition that the local authority shall not 'provide facilities of any description except in cases where it appears to them that the facilities already existing are inadequate or unsatisfactory'.

These powers include one to enter into agreements with other authorities in connection with these facilities. They also include powers to make byelaws eg about boats on a lake, and section 13 of the above Act of 1968 states that such byelaws can take account of the safety of persons resorting to the lake, regulating sports which affect those boats and also, and not least, conserving the amenity and natural beauty of the lake and preventing excessive nuisance from the noise. So the authority can specify the use of silencers if appropriate, the regulation of boats, rules of management, speed limits, as well as charges by the authority. The byelaws can impose different provisions for different parts of such a lake and also for different seasons of the year.

The National Park wardens are empowered to enter both land and water to secure compliance with such provisions; local authorities are encouraged to work jointly in both making and enforcing them.

The seaside

A local authority can make byelaws to regulate public bathing at the seaside (Public Health Act 1936 section 231). Such byelaws would normally deal with times and places for bathing, location of huts or tents, life saving appliances, and the navigation of pleasure boats in relation to bathing places.

The foreshore is that part of the seashore which lies between high and low water marks of ordinary spring tides. It is often owned by the Crown or the Duchies, in Cornwall and Lancaster. The National Trust is also owner of many miles of our coast. This aspect of the law can be important if a local authority wishes to control activities on the foreshore. Taking shingle was the subject of a case at Margate, when the foreshore owner legally prevented this activity; he also prevented bathing huts being placed on the foreshore.[11]

A local authority near The Wash took similar action in the courts to prevent a person from taking mussels from a scalp or bed on the coast.[12]

A third case may be of interest in so far as it secured a court declaration to prevent a public meeting from being held on the foreshore. This is reported in the case of *Llandudno U.D.C. v Woods* (1899)[13].

In these diverse ways, local authorities have useful legal powers to help in regulating seaside activities which call for that means of control.

Wildlife protection

The Wildlife and Countryside Act of 1981 now contains the consolidated code of law for the protection of birds, animals and plants.

Local authorities are given power to take proceedings for the various offences created by this Act (section 25). Local authorities are also placed under a duty to publicise, especially to children, the provisions of the Act of 1981, including Orders of the Secretary of State about the protected species.

Birds

There was a series of Acts preceding the Act of 1981 and their main provisions are now re-enacted as follows:

> It is an offence to kill, injure or take away a wild bird (Act of 1981 section 1); disturb them or their young while in or near their nests; or take or destroy their eggs.

The Act then lists some 70 species of wild birds to be protected in this way and, for the offences described, provides for a fine on conviction.

The Act does list exceptions to the general prohibitions thus set out. These relate to actions outside the close season (generally February to September).

They also extend to landowners in relation to thirteen species of birds considered to do damage, eg crows, gulls and magpies. Their killing is not an offence by such persons if done in the interests of public health, to prevent the spread of disease or to prevent serious damage to livestock, crops or agricultural needs.

Finally, certain methods of killing are prohibited, including traps and electric stunning devices.

Animals

The legislative pattern is similar in relation to wild animals. The Act first makes it an offence to kill, injure or take some 40 species, from natterjack toads to otters and red squirrels to swallowtail butterflies (section 9). There are complementary offences for selling or advertising for sale and also for despoiling the dens or natural shelters of these animals. Exceptions are then created, on the same lines as those given above for birds.

Wild plants

It is made an offence also to pick, uproot or destroy some 60 species of wild plants (section 13). It is also an offence to sell or offer for sale such plants, dead or alive.

There are two other interesting rules in the Act:

1 In proceedings, a plant is deemed to be a wild plant, until the contrary is proved.
2 It is a defence to a charge to show that the act was incidental to a lawful operation and could not reasonably have been avoided.

Conclusion

This survey of ten areas of law operated by local authorities is bound to leave a reader with a longing for the time when related subjects can be collected into one Act of Parliament. The current legislation is uneven, spread over many years and, especially with the Public Health Acts, leaves much to be desired in simple tidiness. We have nevertheless tried to arrange the law on these topics systematically to help the reader to see the total picture. One thing is certain, that the particular area of law where change may next occur cannot be predicted. Each of the subjects considered, except allotments, has been the subject of change by Parliament or the Courts in recent years and further changes can only be expected in the future, as leisure services are adapted to a swiftly changing society.

Notes

1 Local authorities have powers to make byelaws to suppress nuisances and have been encouraged recently by the Home Office to use these to

prescribe ways of dealing with dog droppings (Local Government Act 1972 section 235).

2 *Kruse v Johnson* (1898) 2 QB 91.
3 *Burnley B. C. v England* (1979) 77 LGR 277.
4 *Hall v Beckenham Corporation* (1949) 1 AER 423.
5 Unless the best consideration is obtained (section 123); this is not too easy to establish.
6 eg Re Sutton Common, Wimborne (1982) 2 AER 92.
7 *Harwood v Borough of Reigate and Banstead* (1980) 43 P&CR 336.
8 *Mixnam's Properties v Chertsey U.D.C.* (1965) AC 735.
9 *Esdell Caravan Parks Ltd v Hemel Hempstead U.D.C.* (1965) 3 AER 737.
10 SI 1985 No 1065.
11 *Laird v Briggs* (1880) ChD 440.
12 *Loose v Castle* (1978) 41 P&CR 19.
13 *Llandudno U.D.C. v Woods* (1899) 2 Ch 705.

3 Property problems

Nuisances

The legal term 'nuisance' is a little confusing, for it is used for three separate areas of law: statutory, public and private. Two of them are slight and will not detain us long; the third demands a fuller treatment.

Statutory nuisances

These are created by statute. The Public Health Act 1936 (section 92) lays down six items as capable of being a statutory nuisance, viz premises in such a state as to be prejudicial to health or a nuisance, an animal kept in such a place or manner as to have the same effect, likewise an accumulation or deposit, likewise dust or smell from industrial processes, likewise a workplace, on account of inadequate ventilation, or dirtiness, or overcrowding, and lastly, a catchall, 'any other matter declared by this Act'.

From this starting point, other statutes have created statutory nuisances, such as section 6 of the Clean Air Act 1968, in relation to certain categories of smoke. This is because the Public Health Act 1936 provides a basic procedure for serving an Abatement Notice on the owner or occupier of offending premises, taking them before the Magistrates Court should they not comply and then pursuing the matter with a Nuisance Order if they continue to show defiance (*see* Part III of that Act of 1936).

It is the local authority, in its capacity as a public health authority, which usually enforces these provisions. Further, the statute which creates the offence also creates a defence. This, in general terms, is to the effect that the 'best practicable means' have been used in order to avoid committing the offence in question. This clearly allows a defendant to question the practicality of using particularly expensive equipment, eg filter throats in industrial chimneys, to eliminate certain gases or smoke.

Public nuisances

These are nuisances, which, though not statutory nuisances as described above, are problems for the community. A recent case defined the test as being whether they 'materially affect the comfort and the convenience of the life of a class of Her Majesty's subjects'. Whether that class is large enough is a question of fact in the light of the particular circumstances. Examples of this sort of public nuisance are a pop festival, quarrying to the discomfort of nearby villagers or allowing oil to wash from the sea onto a beach. A local authority or the Attorney General usually initiate the legal process to restrain the nuisance; it is in this situation that the public nuisance is treated as a crime.

If it should have caused special damage to an individual, over and above the damage caused to the general community, then the individual citizen is entitled to initiate the legal proceedings to restrain the nuisance. If successful, he might be granted an injunction and/or damages.

Private nuisances

We turn now to private nuisances, which are by far the most common of the three classes we are describing.

A private nuisance arises when the use of his land by one person causes significant damage to his neighbour, in circumstances where it is actionable. A private nuisance is a tort, a civil wrong, between neighbouring land-owners. It can be caused by smell, noise, as by a music teacher working at all hours in her house, or by water, or by overhanging tree branches or by spreading tree roots which dry out the neighbour's land and cause subsidence to buildings, to take a few examples.

In a famous recent case, householders brought proceedings for nuisance against a neighbouring cricket club. They were annoyed by the frequency with which balls were struck into their property and sometimes broke windows or endangered people. This was the case of *Miller v Jackson* (1977)[1] relating to a cricket field at Burnopfield in Durham and may be of particular interest to readers. The principles could be applied to football grounds, speedway tracks, boat racing lakes or even golf courses.

The case was the culmination of efforts by the club over the years to cure the problem. They had built a wire mesh fence fifteen feet high and thereby reduced the number of trespassing balls to thirteen in three years. Furthermore, the club had been in existence for 70 years, whilst the plaintiff's house had been built only four years before the lawsuit. The house boundary was 200 feet from the nearest crease, whilst their house was 260 feet away.

The lengthy judgements in the Court of Appeal, after extensive argument, gave judgement for the club, on the main issue of an injunction. This overturned a decision in the lower Court. On the other hand, £400 damages was awarded to the householder. The reports are a seed bed of the law for this class of case in modern times.

We may summarise the rules relating to this tort of private nuisance as follows:

1 The interference with the plaintiff's land must be significant.
2 It is no defence to say: You came to the nuisance.
3 Things naturally on the land, like trees, can still lead to their owner causing

a nuisance to his neighbour, if the consequential damage is foreseeable and can be avoided. When the roots of a lime tree caused subsidence of a neighbour's house and the court found that the damage could have been avoided, then the tree owner was liable. In another case, horse chestnut tree roots also caused subsidence. There the Court accepted evidence that this was not foreseeable to the reasonable owner and he won his case.

4 A person making natural use of his land does not become liable to his neighbour in nuisance simply because that neighbour decides to use his own land for some activity which calls for extra sensitive restraint on the nearby land. So, a mink farmer failed in an action for nuisance against his neighbour when allegedly noisy activities harmed the minks during the whelping season.

5 Another example of an activity nuisance could be the occupiers. In one case gypsies were found to be a nuisance to neighbours. It was the local authority on whose land the gypsies were located and the only real issue before the court was whether the Council's letting of the land still kept them knowledgeable and thus liable for what was going on there.[2]

Occupier liability

a Lawful and unlawful visitors. The Occupiers Liability Acts 1957 and 1984

b Safety of Sports Grounds Acts of 1975 and 1987

This is an important branch of the law for all leisure service managers. The properties they man, from public parks and recreation grounds to sports centres and swimming pools, are designed to be visited and used by the public. There was a time when these visitors were graded according to their status in law, as licensees, invitees or persons with a contract and finally, trespassers. Nowadays we have a code of law contained in the Occupiers Liability Act of 1957 which deals with visitors *lawfully* on the occupier's land and also the complementary Act of 1984, in relation to visitors *unlawfully* on that land, namely trespassers.

This is a subject where it may be said that broadly speaking, the law reflects common sense. One does take greater pains to secure the comfort and safety of a guest coming to share a meal, than of the casual caller soliciting money by selling flags for a charity, or perhaps trying to sell double glazing to a reluctant householder. The swimming pool manager will feel more responsible for paying customers than for random strollers in the grounds.

Nevertheless the Courts have uncovered many knotty points in this branch of the law which must be unravelled. It will be convenient to deal first with the occupiers of general premises and, secondly, to turn to the special problems of sports grounds. They have been the subject of two Acts of Parliament in 1975 and in 1987, the latter after the tragedies at the Bradford football ground and the Heysel stadium.

The occupier of general premises

Lawful visitors

The occupier's liability is grouped in the major text books as part of the law of negligence. This is a useful clue to the heart of the legal duty laid upon the occupiers of property in what is called 'the common duty of care'. This is contained in the above Act of 1957 and is in these terms:

> The common duty of care is a duty to take such care as in all the circumstances of the case is reasonable to see that the visitor will be reasonably safe in using the premises for the purpose for which he is invited or permitted by the occupier to be there. (section 2)

We comment on the points to which this definition has given rise:

The visitor The law allows for the fact that children require a greater degree of care from the occupier than adults. 'An occupier must be prepared for children to be less careful than adults' is the welcome and lucid statement of this principle in section 2 above. In practice this means that the occupier must take pains to keep an 'allurement' out of their way. This could be machinery – a railway turntable in a leading case – or apparatus in a multigym, if potentially harmful to youngsters. Whilst entitled to expect very young children to be accompanied by elders to guard them, the occupier must still beware of tolerating children encroaching on something with concealed danger. He could otherwise be found to have permitted them to go to that place.

The cases show that occupiers are penalised if they tacitly encourage children to go where they are forbidden and then do not protect them from dangers. The hazard might be a shiny and slippery floor or perhaps an open air swimming pool, whose depth varied with the incoming and outgoing tide. In one case the injury was a young person's hand caught in a moving lift and in another it happened after sliding down a grassy slope with broken glass at the bottom. It is over 50 years since Glasgow Corporation were held liable for the death of a 7 year old boy who ate from brightly coloured but poisonous berries in a public park.[3] The principle is still active and reinforced in the courts: 'allurements' are to be looked at through children's spectacles.

Apart from this well-developed law about children, visitors can include the window cleaner or the fireman or the decorator, who may be expected to know any peculiarities of the premises if guided by the occupier but who, initially, need to be told of loose treads or unlit back passages and other hazards.

Surprisingly, a special provision in the Act of 1957 (section 1) excludes from the category of 'visitor', the person in a National Park, under an access agreement.

Limiting the duty The Act of 1957 allows the occupier to limit his duty of care. He may 'extend, restrict, modify or exclude "his duty to visitors" by agreement or otherwise'. A sufficiently clear notice in the right place can achieve this limitation, though only to the extent that it is reasonable. The Courts are alert to protect a plaintiff, where he has little chance to avoid a danger in reality.

The above remarks do not apply to the visitor under contract, eg a window cleaner or the hirer of a room. Another Act, the Unfair Contract Terms Act 1977, specifically forbids the exclusion in such cases of the common duty of care.

Risks accepted by the visitor It is common practice to get visitors to, say, a tower viewing platform, to sign an indemnity for the occupier before being allowed to those parts of the premises. This complies with another part of section 2 in the Act of 1957. This relieves the occupier of liability under the common duty of care when the visitor has 'willingly accepted' a risk. This principle has a large application to the playing of games and particularly sports in premises managed in the leisure services. These activities involve an acceptance of risk from other players and when the normal incidents of the activity in question are not exceeded, the occupier is not legally liable.

The premises The Act of 1957 complicates this aspect a little by defining the relevant premises as including 'a fixed or movable structure, including any vessel, vehicle or aircraft'. Diving boards and playground equipment are clearly fixed structures for this purpose.

Unlawful visitors

The Act of 1984 mentioned above was a successor to the Act of 1957, which had been praised for codifying most of the principles affecting the legal duties of the occupier to his visitors.

However, it is doubtful if the 1984 Act has done more than re-write a set of legal principles and leave open several points of importance in our law about trespassers. The trespasser is admittedly on the premises at his own risk. He is the last person to have a right to complain if the premises are not as safe as he thought they were. He has no right to be there.

In those circumstances, it is only when the occupier: (1) knows of danger on his land, eg a loosely covered pit awaiting the return of workmen or an unguarded excavation for roads or other works; (2) knows that trespassers are on his land or are about to come, and (3) that they do not know of the danger, that he has the duty to warn them or otherwise take reasonable steps to avoid their falling into the danger in question.

This seems, with respect, to say in longer terms that he must not knowingly set a trap, which was the old principle applied by the courts.

Trespassing children This duty is heightened when children are the trespassers. This is because the duty is about the steps the reasonable occupier might be expected to take and, as in the general situation discussed above, this inevitably throws on him a special duty to alert those who will not appreciate what adults might understand quite easily, even if as the Law Reform Committee said in their report, which led to this Act, they are all 'uninvited entrants'.

Occupier of sports grounds

The Act of 1975

Sometimes a statement of law is best understood in the light of its development. That is the case with this area of law, which has undergone rapid change in recent years.

Until 1975 there was no statute about sports grounds as such, though building regulations had references to specific buildings. Accidents at the

Brooklands motor car race track or a football ground were dealt with on the basis of common law principles about occupiers and their visitors. The Safety of Sports Grounds Act 1975 however broke new ground and followed recommendations of the Wheatley Committee in 1972 (66 spectators had died shortly before in a disaster at Ibrox Park).

The pattern of control set up by this Act of 1975 may be summarised as follows:

1 Regarding a 'stadium' as comprising a sports arena 'substantially surrounded' by spectator accommodation, the Act was aimed at such a stadium if it had a capacity for 10,000 or more spectators.
2 The Secretary of State (the Home Secretary) could designate such a stadium; its managers were then under a legal duty to obtain a Safety Certificate for it from the local authority.
3 The Safety Certificate would normally state a limit to the number of permitted spectators. It would also say how many occasions were covered or it might be for an indefinite number. It would then give details about exits, entrances, means of access, crash barriers and means of escape in case of fire.
4 The Act also set up procedures to deal with amendments to Safety Certificates, appeals against refusals to grant them, alterations to stadiums and entry by the police and building authority representatives to inspect the premises.
5 The Act created an offence for not having a required Safety Certificate or for breaking its requirements.
6 A defence was also created if the Court was satisfied that the holder took all reasonable precautions and exercised all due diligence to comply with the Certificate.
7 Duplication with other Acts of Parliament was to be avoided by providing that sections of other Acts would not apply whilst a Safety Certificate was in force.
8 There was an emergency procedure available to obtain an Order from a Magistrates Court about crowd limits.

The Popplewell Report[4]

The Popplewell Committee of Inquiry was set up after the fire disaster at the Bradford football ground in 1985. (As the Heysel Stadium disaster in Belgium occurred shortly after the Committee of Inquiry had been established that stadium was visited and implications of the collapse of the separating wall were taken into account also.) After taking a great deal of evidence, the Popplewell Committee reached the following main conclusions in its Interim and Final Report(s) (referred to here as the Popplewell Report):

1 The Act of 1975 was too limited in the grounds it dealt with; the problem of crowd safety was serious at many other sports grounds.
2 The distinction should be abolished between a stadium, as defined above, and a sports ground, viz a place where sports took place before spectators in the open air. Sports ground should be the general legal term.
3 The Popplewell Inquiry heard a lot about the team of officers who had to work together on the response to an application for a Safety Certificate under the Act of 1975. The Popplewell Report declined to say who should be the lead officer in such an exercise. It did however ask for a model Safety Certificate to be drafted, in order to overcome problems found in the differing levels of detail put into sample certificates studied by the Committee of Inquiry.

4 The three main potential hazards at a sports ground were fire risk, structural failure and crowd control. The legislation should be flexible enough to cater for grounds where not all three elements were present.

5 Rugby league, rugby union and cricket were the three spectator sports which were, after football, thought to display the risks for which legislation had to be framed.

6 Because of its anxiety that one authority should be responsible to inspect and certify sports grounds, the Popplewell Report recommended that all sports grounds with accommodation for 500 or more spectators should come under the Fire Precautions Act. In the same spirit the Report urged that structural risks should be handled by one authority, though the Report did not specify which this should be.

7 Because evidence showed that there were fire risks, the Report recommended that indoor sports facilities also, where 500 or more spectators were provided for, should come under the Fire Precautions Act for fire certificates.

The Popplewell Report came before Parliament and gave rise to two important steps:

a The new Act of 1987, and
b The revision of the Green Guide issued by the Home Office.

Act of 1987
The Fire Safety and Safety of Places of Sports Act 1987

The Act is in five Parts and is being brought into force in phases. Part II about safety at sports grounds, is being brought into operation first. It has seven sections and abolishes the earlier distinction between stadiums and sports grounds; it allows the Home Secretary to fix the qualifying capacity, rather than embody 10,000 or another figure in the Act; it also tightens up the law about prohibition notices, enforcement and inspectors.

Part III is also being brought into force in 1988; it relates to the safety of stands at sports grounds and contains sixteen sections. Some of its provisions are detailed and unsuitable for summary here., Furthermore, regulations are to supplement the statute. However, some new provisions should be noted and then the Act studied for the detail:

1 A stand which provides covered accommodation for 500 or more spectators in a ground which has not hitherto been designated, now needs a Safety Certificate from the local authority.

2 Such a stand is called a 'Regulated Stand'.

3 It is the duty of the local authority to decide which stands at sports grounds in their area are Regulated Stands and to issue Safety Certificates under the statutory procedure for them.

4 Safety Certificates may in future be *general*, if for an indefinite period, or *special*, if for a specified number of activities or occasions.

5 The issue of certificates is to follow a procedure which includes a preliminary determination about a stand being a Regulated Stand and then, after a two month period for representations, a final determination embodied in the Safety Certificate for that stand.

6 Safety Certificates can be amended, repealed, replaced and transferred and there is also an appeal system which may give rise to some of these modifications to the Safety Certificate as originally issued.

7 Appeals go to the Magistrates Court and orders of those courts can be further appealed to the Crown Courts (section 30).
8 There are new offences for using a stand without a current Safety Certificate and for breaching conditions in such a Certificate.
9 Offences may be punished by fine or in some cases by imprisonment. Defences are also provided, based upon ignorance of the true situation about a Regulated Stand or on having taken all reasonable precautions to avoid the breach in question.

Generally these parts follow the recommendations of the Popplewell Report.

Part IV introduces indoor sports licences. These will be phased into force. They are for 'sports entertainment' but, whilst of general application to sports complexes, do not apply if the sporting event which constitutes the 'entertainment' is not the principal purpose for which the premises are used on the occasion in question.

Part V has a small number of miscellaneous provisions about entertainment licences. These include power to charge a fee for dealing with a variation in the terms of the licence. In addition, the Royal Albert Hall is no longer exempt from the entertainment provisions in the Local Government Act 1982.

Lastly, Part I is not yet in force. It contains eighteen sections in relation to fire safety; these amend earlier provisions in the Fire Precautions Act 1971. In particular, they allow more flexibility to the fire authority about fire certificates, charging fees for certification work, power for the Secretary of State to issue Codes of Practice, the use of Improvement Notices (section 7) to remedy contraventions of fire certificates and also appeals and offences.

The Green Guide
This is the Home Office publication which gives detailed advice about safety measures needed at sports grounds. Originally produced after the Wheatley Report of 1972, this Guide has been completely revised in the light of the Popplewell Report and was re-published in 1986.

Its detailed guidance relates to entrances and exits, the structure of stands and buildings, stairways and ramps, the terraces, crush barriers and hand rails and perimeter walls and fences. In addition, the Green Guide discusses management responsibility, inspections and tests, stewarding and crowd control, ground capacity estimates and flow rates for the crowd.

It is clearly obligatory reading for all leisure service managers involved in any aspect of sports ground management.

Estates and interests

Leisure service managers in day to day work may well find that they deal with tenants or licensees within the portfolio of property for which they are responsible. These may be park keepers who are tenants of a house or lodge within a park or estate. They may be caretakers of swimming pools or sports centres, who have a flat in the corner of a large building. They may in some extensive estate, not yet handed over to the National Trust, have a tenant farmer or smallholder.

Apart from such tenants, they may have to oversee the licensee of advertisement hoardings, or ice cream kiosks, or part of a sports centre cafeteria. Against such a background, what is the legal difference between a tenant and a licensee? Is there a troublesome restrictive covenant over part of some land or a neighbour's rights of light or way or support? Finally, has he a problem wall? Hence we turn to:

1 Legal ownership of land
2 Third party interests
3 Landlords, tenants and licences
4 Walls

Legal ownership of land

The owner of freehold land in this country is said in law to hold that land 'in fee simple'. This expression has come down to us from the feudal system, under which, after the Norman Conquest, land was divided into estates and, after many transfers of ownership, into small plots suitable for individual ownership and use.

The *fee* is the estate held by the complete or absolute owner. The word actually indicates that it can be inherited; to say that a man holds the house in fee means that in law it is for him and his heirs. On the historical footing that the Crown owned all land, it was the estate in fee to the Crown which was the most complete ownership possible. *Simple* is, in this context, a word which in law describes the ownership as being free from conditions, such as a limited line of descent, say, only through females, on death of the estate holder.

Only two legal estates

This absolute ownership is one of two estates which can exist in our system of land holding; this is by virtue of the Law of Property Act 1925. That was a watershed in our land law, by which a clutter of different sorts of land holding was greatly simplified. The second and only other legal estate in land permitted by that Act of 1925 is the term of years absolute, ie a full blown lease.

Ownership 'in fee simple' is, strictly, rounded off by three more words: *absolute in possession*. These describe the total and immediate nature of the ownership. Some ownerships are carved out of a larger land holding and may be designed to come into existence in full in the future, perhaps on someone's death, perhaps on attaining a specified age, such as 18 or 21 years. Those sort of fetters do not apply to the fee simple absolute in possession.

Third party interests

Easements

An easement is an interest attached to and benefitting one plot of land and exercised over another plot. It can for instance be a right of way or a right of light or a right of support. It could be a right to place advertisements on that land or to water your cattle in another person's stream.

It is a legal interest when made by deed and held in fee simple or, in the same way as a lease, for a term of years. If for a lesser period, eg for life, it is called an equitable interest.

When land is conveyed formally to a person to hold in fee simple, that conveyance, without specifically saying so, includes all easements attached to the land.

An easement is to be distinguished from the right, curiously called a profit à prendre (a right to take something). This is the right which covers the taking of turf, or timber, or pasturing cattle or taking sand or fish from someone else's land. With an easement, you do not *take* anything from that other land: you simply make a permitted *use* of it.

Restrictive covenants

Whilst the easement benefits your land, the restrictive covenant is a disadvantage to your land. It defines the restriction to which your land is subject. Perhaps it is to stop your land being used for trade or for the sale of alcohol. Possibly it prevents you from putting up a building more than two storeys high on your land.

To be enforceable in law, it must be clear in its concept and in its language; so also must be the identity of the land which it is to benefit. Further, to prevail against a legal estate, it must be registered in the proper register as a Land Charge.[5]

Changes in the locality   Because the character of a district changes, some restrictive covenants which were sensible when they were made become inappropriate in the course of time. To meet that situation, the Law of Property Act 1925 section 84 allows a Court to modify or even cancel a restrictive covenant, if duly satisfied that changes in the neighbourhood justify that course of action.

In the law of both easements and restrictive covenants, there are numerous rules and technical details which are not discussed here; we are simply giving a general picture.

Landlords, tenants and licences

Against the background sketched in the introductory paragraph, we shall now look at the law about residential tenancies, business tenancies and agricultural tenancies. This will be followed by a discussion of the differences between tenancies and licences.

Residential lettings

The owner of a house or flat may let its *possession* to a tenant, without parting with the *ownership*. This letting, if by deed, can create a lease which is a legal estate, ie a term of years, normally three years or more. On the other hand, if concluded as an agreement under signature, usually called under hand, it can create a tenancy which could be on a weekly, monthly or yearly private or public sector. The main feature in law is the protected security enjoyed by business tenants. This for example puts the landlord to proof of why he wishes to recover possession of the premises against the wish of the tenant. In law this takes the form of settling the issue of whether or not the Court should allow the tenant to have a new tenancy when his present one expires.

'Business' The definition of 'business' in the Act of 1954 is 'a trade, profession or employment and includes any activity carried on by a body of persons'. This was deemed sufficiently wide for the Courts to hold a tennis club to be a business within it.

Exclusions Nevertheless there are exclusions and these extend to the service occupancy, licensed premises, premises which are in part residential and also commercial licences such as the ice cream kiosk or the promenade take-away stall.

Within the strict time limits set out in this legislation, the landlord can recover possession on the ground of breaches of his covenants by the tenant and also if he should need to demolish or reconstruct the property or wish to occupy it himself.

Assignments The landlord of a business tenancy has not a great deal of room to manoeuvre when presented by his tenant with a request to assign the tenancy; this difficulty stems from the provision in the Act of 1954 (section 19) which says that he is not to refuse such a request 'unreasonably'.

Agricultural tenancies
These are yet one more class, out of eight in all, where legislation now provides some security of tenure for the tenant. Each code is different and the resulting law is, inevitably, complex.

The main feature of this class for leisure service managers may be that it has no application to local authority houses. Again the type of agricultural letting most frequently met in this country is probably the tied cottage and this is not normally a problem for the above class of readers. In the circumstances it seems desirable simply to mention a series of sign posts for those who have to travel along the roads they designate.

1 The **Agricultural Holdings Act 1948** gives protection to the tenant of an agricultural holding, being one used commercially for agriculture. Its code centres on the need for a twelve month notice to quit such a holding. This has to be served at the appropriate time of the year and it can give rise to an issue before the Agricultural Land Tribunal about the merits of granting possession to the landlord. The safeguarding of continuity of cultivation of the agricultural holding is an important consideration.

2 The **Rent (Agriculture) Act 1975** is the guide on security of tenure for tenants of non local authority houses occupied in connection with agriculture.

3 The **Protection from Eviction Act 1977** section 4 should be studied if the manager becomes involved in recovery of possession from the tenant of a house occupied in connection with agriculture. The hearing which may

basis and intended, if all goes well, to continue indefinitely. As distinct from the formal lease, it can be terminated by notice to quit. The lease would run its course.

Terms of tenancy   The provisions to be included in the usual tenancy agreement of a dwelling will be the rent, the arrangements for its payment, the permitted use, the description of the premises let, any restriction on use or upon encroaching on the neighbours' property to clean windows or point a gable wall. The agreement will specify the names of the parties and who pays the rates. These are the basic terms. The tenants will agree to pay the rent and obey the stipulations set out and cause no nuisance to his neighbours. The landlord will agree to let the property and allow the tenant to have the quiet possession and peaceable enjoyment of the property, as it is traditionally described.

This is the very basic structure of the normal tenancy agreement. Almost every term mentioned can give rise to difficulties of interpretation and there are many cases in the reports about the construction of words that the parties used and as many again on their intentions about matters on which the agreement is silent. The Courts have conjectured about the intentions of landlords and tenants in homely phrases such as: If we had asked, as they signed the agreement, 'Did you mean there would be no objection to dogs, cats and canaries?' they would have replied, Of course'.

Yet for all the problem tenancies, there are millions which do not cause problems.

The description so far given has to be supplemented by an awareness of statute law. Rent Restrictions Acts have limited in varying degrees of complexity the amount of rent which may lawfully be charged for a residential letting (*see now* the Rent Act 1977 and the Housing Act 1980). The Housing Acts have made it unlawful to let a house as a dwelling which is unfit for that use – and for example the absence of safe ventilation in the only bedroom has been held to make such a house unfit. A tenant whose initial tenancy has been terminated can, on remaining in occupation, become a 'statutory tenant', with a personal right to occupy and keep paying the rent.

Recovery of possession from a tenant who, despite proper termination, declines to leave, can be achieved with the help of a court order. This is usually the County Court and the order is normally made only if the Court is satisfied that a breach of the tenant's obligations has occurred or one of twenty other grounds for a possession order are made out. These include the need to replace the occupant by another employee of the landlord – a situation that may well be met in the leisure services. Further, a recent statute introduces Shorthold, being a tenancy of one to five years and which has certain advantages to landlords for the purpose of recovering possession.

The public housing sector has several special provisions in comparison with the private sector. These include a greater freedom in fixing rents and also some different grounds for recovering possession.

Business tenancies
These come under the Landlord and Tenant Act 1954, whether in the

follow service of the notice to quit may be necessary to determine the question of possession; it will reach a decision only after hearing evidence about the efficient management of agricultural land, possible damage caused to the property and relations of the tenant with his neighbours.

Tenants and licences

It will be apparent that persons holding tenancies of the nature discussed above usually enjoy some protection against arbitrary eviction. This makes it advisable that managers consider with their legal advisers the type of occupancy to be granted, especially when possession of the property may be needed in the foreseeable future. We consider two different forms of licence as options for that situation.

Non-residential licence   Many properties can be put out on a licence which yields regular income and ensures that it is used as desired and yet allows possession to be recovered if development of that locality should be desirable. Park cafeterias, huts and advertisement hoardings are simple examples of lettings suitable for the licence, sometimes called a bare licence. This embodies permission to enter for the stated use, in return for a stipulated payment. The words tenant, rent, notice to quit and the other terminology used in normal tenancy agreements are best avoided. Yet the Courts have said that they look at the substance rather than the form in deciding if the occupation is a tenancy or a licence.

A recent example is instructive. A lady allowed to serve take-away food in the market square at Crook, County Durham on three nights a week was considered by the local authority, as owners of the square, to be on a licence and they gave her one month's notice to move. This was done without warning or reasons. This business was the lady's sole source of livelihood and there had been no complaint about litter or otherwise prior to the termination notice.

The Court said she was entitled to natural justice, as a person on a licence. This meant that she should be heard in her defence before a decision to oust her was taken. Hence the decision of the Wear Valley District Council was quashed on a judicial review in the High Court.[6]

It is emphasised that apart from the difficulties a landowner may encounter by granting a tenancy when a licence would have sufficed, some third party coming on the scene also needs to clarify the position. He will wish to know the position in case he needs to obtain possession.

Service licence   This is the licence granted to the employee who is required to occupy a flat or cottage or house in order to be able to do his job satisfactorily. The unique feature of his occupancy is that it ends when his job ends. The agreement between the parties says as much and in any claim for possession in Court against an employee who continues in occupation in contravention of the agreement, the Court will wish to know of the effectiveness of the notice terminating the employment and not, as in the normal possession case, the details of a notice to quit. The employer in Court would also be expected to show that he needed the house for another employee.

So the chauffeur, the lodge in the forest for the woodman, the sports centre flat all have to be handled with care, not least in the documents accompanying the initial handing over of the key. The usual items that regulate occupation of a dwellinghouse will be in that document, about repairs, rates, insurance, not causing a nuisance, not assigning possession and no alterations to the premises without consent of the owner.

But the service licence – sometimes called occupancy – is meant to be different from, and is in law different from, the tenancy granted by a landlord; it is an occupation insisted upon by an employer. That is why the Courts, in cases on this topic, sometimes use the expression 'the occupation is the occupation of the employer'.

The Courts do not acknowledge the existence of this service licence readily when one comes before them: they need to be convinced. A recent case in 1985 reached the Court of Appeal and exemplifies this cautious attitude. In *Royal Philanthropic Society v County*[7] an employee was granted the occupation of the employer's house and did not give up possession when the employment ended. The Court saw no evidence that the occupation of the house was 'for the better performance of his duties as a servant'. They looked rather to see if the tenure was that of a lodger or a tenant and found a tenancy. In doing so, they differed from a lower Court, which had thought that there was sufficient connection between the job and the house to treat the occupation as a service licence.

Walls

The legal guidelines for dealing with walls and fences may be summarised in this way:

1 If someone has damaged a wall, primarily they are responsible for its repair.
2 If by age or a hurricane, a wall falls and needs repair, it may be a fence wall between two ownerships and the responsibility is borne equally.
3 Often due to their nature, walls carry a history and knowledge of the last repair may be vital.
   a Can it be established from the title deeds and T marks on the deed plan where responsibility lies?
   b Is it perhaps known who built the wall and is, in the absence of conflicting evidence, thus responsible for its repair?
   c Does the construction of the wall, smooth outside and rough on the inside, show that it was intended as a park or other boundary wall built by the park owner, to keep *in* the park?
   d Is it perhaps a retaining wall? If it retains a highway, that authority should accept responsibility for the portion below the road as in law part of the highway. In the absence of other evidence, the portion above the soil, the fence wall as it is called, will be the responsibility of the landowner.
   e If a highway is adjacent, then possibly the highway authority or the landowner is deriving support from land of the other; if enjoyed for a sufficient length of time there may indeed be an easement in the form of a legal right of support. On the other hand, if the adjoining owner needs the wall to keep the soil from falling onto his land, this could give rise to responsibility for repair shared equally.

4 Certain statutes may have a bearing on repairs within the leisure service situation. A closed churchyard may have become a lawn cemetery and thus under the responsibility of the local authority. The boundary wall would be expected to go along with the cemetery under the Burial Act 1900 section 10 and the subsequent transfer under the Local Government Act 1972 section 215. Again, the highway authority has power to require fencing of a danger adjoining a highway, by notice under the Highways Act 1980 (section 163). Lastly, if the action is needed against a person who has failed to honour a legal covenant to erect a fence, perhaps when land ownership was divided on a sale, then the Limitation Act 1980 can be relevant. It has a twelve year limit on actions in the Courts based upon such a deed.

Conclusion

The three aspects of land law which we have been considering are fundamental to those engaged in leisure services management. One needs only to instance the recourse in recent years, in order to obtain speedier finance for hard pressed local authorities, to sale and lease-back arrangements, in order to underline the continuing application of fundamental principles in this branch of our law.

A recent survey of reforms in land law in 1987 concluded sadly 'The chimera of simplicity looks as far away as ever.'[8]

Notes

1 *Miller v Jackson* (1977) QB 966.
2 *Page Motors v Epson & Ewell B.C.* (1982) LGR 337.
3 *Taylor v Glasgow Corporation* (1922) 1 AC 44.
4 Cmd 4952, HMSO.
5 If the land is registered, you must look in HM Land Registry.
6 *Reg. v Wear Valley D.C. ex parte Binks* (1985) 2 AER 699.
7 *Royal Philanthropic Society v County* (1985) EG 1068.
8 All ER Annual Review 156.

4 Staff problems

4.1 Negligence

We begin with a classic statement of the general principle:

> The rule that you are to love your neighbour becomes, in law, you must not injure your neighbour and the lawyer's question 'Who is my neighbour?' receives a restricted reply.
>
> You must take reasonable care to avoid acts and omissions which you can reasonably foresee would be likely to injure your neighbour. Who then, in law, is my neighbour? The answer seems to be – persons who are so closely and directly affected by my act, that I ought reasonably to have them in contemplation as being so affected when I am directing my mind to the acts or omissions which are called in question.

This is part of the judgement of Lord Atkin in the House of Lords in the case of *Donoghue v Stevenson* (1932).[1] A lady, shocked and sickened at finding the apparent remains of a snail in a bottle of ginger beer recently purchased, successfully sued the manufacturers. In contract a person can take action only against the person with whom he has a contract. The case was a breakthrough in recognising the right of action, in a non-contractual situation, of a consumer against a manufacturer, when no intermediate handling of the article might be expected to change its nature before being put to its intended use. (This was clearly before and independent of recent consumer protection legislation.)

So we have, in the normal legal action for negligence, first a duty of care, then the breach of that duty and thirdly damages for injury to a person or damage to property resulting from that breach. The three elements are needed before we have the tort of negligence. So the bricklayer, on the second storey of the new sports centre in course of building has a duty of care. He may drop bricks every day; it is only when damage to property or injury to a person is caused by breach of that duty, the dropping of a brick on them, that duty, breach and damage are complete and an action against the bricklayer lies.

We consider, accordingly, in relation to leisure service managers, first the general duty, then how it works out in practice in dealing with staff. We then deal shortly with the duty in relation to participants in sport, with which the managers are involved, the defences to a negligence claim and finally, in the aftermath of Bradford and Heysel, the Popplewell Report and the Green Guide.

Duty

This is fundamentally to exercise care to avoid acts and omissions which can reasonably be foreseen to be likely to cause damage. ('Damage' is the technical term used for a legal wrong which may be injury to a person, physical damage to property and sometimes emotional or economic injury to other persons.)

It exists according to the circumstances. This means, for instance, that it does not tolerate a lower standard of care from the swimming pool attendant on his first day at work than from a lady attendant occupying the same post with twenty years' experience at the job. The duty to spot and assist the swimmer in difficulties is the same for both.

But the duty is defined in relation to the current standard of the ordinary skilled man exercising and professing to have that special skill. This means, for instance, keeping abreast of the appropriate journals for people in that occupation. If, as an example, there are two recognised life saving techniques, the proper use of one, even if unsuccessful, will not carry legal blame. But, said a judge in a leading case, 'that does not mean that a (medical) man can obstinately and pig-headedly carry on with some old technique, if it has been proved to be contrary to what is really substantially the whole of informed (medical) opinion'.[2]

Thus, as knowledge changes so must skill and so also must legal accountability. Lord Denning gave us one epigram on this point. 'We must not,' he said, 'look at a 1947 accident with 1954 spectacles.' Another example is to be found in the growing recognition that deafness is caused by hitherto unsuspected industrial noises.

If these comments suggest an expansion of the duty of legal care, then the reader may find comfort in another group of cases which limit that expansion. A person physically close to a nasty accident suffered by a near relative, may have a legal claim in their own right against the person responsible for the accident.[3] On the other hand, the same relative, a long way off at the time of the accident and aware of the details only at second hand, may not have such a right. They would not be within that group of persons whom the law might hold the perpetrator of the accident to have had in mind as affected by his action, within the test set out above in *Dohoghue v Stevenson*. This branch of law is called 'remoteness of damage'.

Reasonably foreseeable

It may be helpful to illustrate from two cases about football and cricket, how the phrase 'reasonably foreseeable' in the Donoghue case is interpreted in the courts.

In *Bolton v Stone* (1951)[4] a lady walking in a road adjacent to a cricket ground was injured by a ball struck more lustily than usual. The ground was the club ground of Cheetham Cricket Club and cricket had been played there for 90 years. There was a fence 7 feet high round the ground; a pronounced slope meant that the top of this fence was 17 feet higher than the pitch at the point where the ball crossed it. It was moreover 78 yards from the striker to the fence and 100 yards to the point where the plaintiff was hit. Whilst one witness spoke of balls coming into his premises five or six times in recent years, club members could remember no comparable incident. They said the hit, a straight drive, was exceptional. After hearing the evidence, the Court said the possibility of such injury was not one a reasonable man would have contemplated. The cricket club were successful, the Court agreeing that no special fencing or other protection for highway users was required to discharge their legal duty.

In *Hilder v Associated Portland Cement Manufacturers Ltd* (1961),[5] however, a motor cyclist was struck by a football kicked from adjoining grounds by boys allowed to play there by the owners. The Court decided that the likelihood of injury in this way was a real one; it should have been foreseen and the injured plaintiff won his case.

Lastly in this general section, we draw attention to the difference which the character of the plaintiff may make. A child requires greater care than an adult. A disabled person needs special attention in relation to his disability. In this, the law coincides with common sense; though it may not always be easy to discharge that legal duty of special care.

We turn now to the other four special aspects of negligence.

In relation to staff

An employer can become liable for negligence in this field in two quite separate ways. The first is where he is liable for some negligence *of* his staff because they are doing what he has employed them to do. This is called vicarious liability. The second case is where he is liable *to* his staff, because he has not carried out some legal duty he owes to them. We take these in turn.

Vicarious liability

There are three main principles in this field:

    1 Generally an employer becomes liable for the negligence of his employee, giving rise to a third party claim for damages, where that negligence took place in the course of his employment.
    2 Where however the negligence took place outside the course of the employment, the employer is not so liable. This is so, even if the opportunity to commit the negligent act was created by the employment.
    3 The freedom of the employer from liability is even more clear if the negligence occurs whilst the employee was, to use a historic legal phrase, 'on a frolic of his own'.

We now illustrate these important principles with some examples:
(i) During a high kick by a dancer doing his turn at the Wood Green Empire the heel came off his shoe, flew through the air and injured a member of the audience in the face. The Court found that the defendants, who had con-

tracted with the theatre to provide a number of artistic turns, were not in law 'employers' of The Four Playboys, the group involved in the mishap. The claim failed; even more, the judge did not find negligence in the actual dancer or his routine.[6]

(ii) A cub member of a scout group went to Whipsnade Zoo. He got away from the adults in charge, crawled between the two fences surrounding the lions' cage, was mauled and died. The Court held that the Boy Scouts Association were not vicariously liable for the acts of scout masters and cub mistresses. They also held, on the facts, that the cub mistress was not negligent in letting the cubs split into groups.[7]

(iii) A workman going legitimately by car to get tools, or a meal, whilst on an outside job, had an accident and ran over the plaintiff's husband, who was killed. The workman should have used his employer's vehicle and not his own. The Court said this was not important. What mattered was that he was engaged on his employer's business and the employer was liable for the consequences of his negligence.[8]

(iv) Sometimes the Courts have to draw a distinction between the 'authorised province of operation' and subsequent events. Thus a dance hall steward struck an unruly customer in the dance hall and the employer was liable. But when the steward continued by going outside and hitting the customer again, the employer was not liable. It was, said the Court, 'a private act of retaliation'.[9]

(v) In a leading case, a solicitor's managing clerk was held out by his employers as trustworthy to handle particular transactions. In one matter he was fraudulent, the client suffered in consequence and the solicitor was held to be responsible for the resulting damages.[10]

We cannot pretend that this branch of the law is easy. Lord Denning once said that it was baffling. He also said that it was the nature of the employer's obligation to the plaintiff that was critical. A 1987 case has reiterated the dividing line between 'in' or 'not in' the course of employment. A cleaning contractor employed a cleaner to clean an office. The cleaner used the office telephone to make personal calls to the tune of over £1000. As this act was completely outside the terms of the cleaner's employment, the employer was not liable.[11]

Direct liability to his employees
The second class of case may be dealt with briefly. The employer is liable to his employee for his own negligence, as he is to other people. This negligence may take the form of providing faulty plant or defective materials or incompetent superiors, such as foremen.

Additionally, this negligence may arise from the employer's responsibility for an unsafe system of working. Many of the reported cases on this point come from industrial situations or stevedores loading ships. The principle can however easily be called into play in a leisure service situation if say the method of cleaning or draining the swimming pool was faulty and injury resulted. Other examples might relate to the raising or lowering of equipment in a sports centre or any other potentially dangerous operations.

Negligence in relation to participants in sport

A manager of a sports centre or swimming pool may become involved in engaging sportsmen for a display or an exhibition match. In this setting, he could become responsible in law if, by his negligence in relation to the condition of the building or the pool, one of the participants is injured. We look at two examples.

Latchford v Spedeworth International Ltd (1984)[12]
The plaintiff was a racing driver who successfully sued the managers of Wimbledon Stadium after suffering injury during hot rod racing events. Near to the inner edge of the track were two concrete flower beds, potentially dangerous to drivers. The stadium owner used a series of small tyres on the ground to mark out the boundary of the racing track. During a race, the car in front of the plaintiff's struck some of these tyres. Some were propelled onto the track and one jammed under the rear axle of the plaintiff's car, causing it to jam and the car was catapulted sideways out of control; the plaintiff suffered a head-on collision with the concrete flower beds. The owner did not then know that large tyres, used as markers, would have been safer. In Court, it was held that though the plaintiff, being familiar with the stadium, had an objective awareness of the flower beds and so could be said to have accepted the risks of their closeness to the track, he did not have 'a full appreciation of the nature and extent of the risk, because of his ignorance of the peril created by the use of the small tyres'. As stated, the plaintiff accordingly succeeded.

Harrison v Vincent (1982)[13]
It was the wording of a test, framed by the Court in this case, that was quoted above. In this case the ground organisers were found liable for an obstruction in a slip road constructed as part of a motor cycle racing circuit near Scarborough. A driver in peril was forced to turn into this slip road and the accident occurred when the plaintiff struck a standing recovery vehicle in this situation. International requirements called for the slip road to be clear for 100 metres adjacent to the circuit but the obstruction was only 30–40 metres from the course. It should have been foreseeable, said the Court, that this obstruction was a potential source of danger.

A case which exonerated the ground owner was *Simms v Leigh R.F.C.* (1969).[14] The plaintiff was injured doing a tackle and blamed the owner for the proximity of a wall to the playing area. He alleged that his head struck this wall during the tackle in question. The Court did not accept either of these contentions.

Defences

There are generally four defences which may be available to a person sued for damages for negligence.

1 *Contributory negligence* involves an allegation by the defendant that the injury suffered by the plaintiff was due in part at least, to his own negligence, eg he may not have worn a safety belt. The plaintiff's negligence

reduces the amount of damages which the defendant has to pay by whatever proportion, eg a quarter or a half, which the Court determines. The Law Reform (Contributory Negligence) Act 1945 governs the details of this matter.

2 *Volenti non fit injuria.* This maxim means that a person who assents to an injury cannot sue for it. So participants in games are expected to accept the normal risks of play in those games, ie none in chess, plenty in rugby football. Likewise spectators are deemed to accept some risks associated with the particular sport. When a puck flew into the crowd during ice hockey at the Harringay Arena the person injured did not succeed in an action against the stadium owner.[15] This is sometimes a subtle area of law, since unexpected risks are not deemed to be accepted. The Latchford case above is one where the defence of *volenti* failed for the reason given.

Again sometimes a bystander injured has acted under a sufficiently strong moral compulsion so that it does not lie in the mouth of the defendant to suggest that he accepted a risk. There is a classic case on this. A policeman was injured in restraining a bolting horse.[16] He acted to protect people including children who were in the path of the horse. The Court said that the plaintiff was responding to an emergency created by the defendant's negligence and thus the plaintiff won his case. It must be said that the Courts are reluctant to see this defence succeed in any but the clearest cases.

3 *Statutory powers.* Many local authorities are leisure services authorities and thus will carry out some of their recreation provision under Acts of Parliament. If damage is caused when statutory powers are properly used, then the authority has a good legal defence. But if the powers are used negligently, this is a different matter. Then there is full legal liability. The House of Lords had the opportunity to review this part of the law in 1970 in a case, which whilst involving yachts, was fundamentally about the responsibility of the Home Office when managing a Borstal institution. What happened was that seven boys escaped from this custody, in Dorset, seized a yacht and set sail. However, in the course of this adventure, they damaged the plaintiff's boat. He was successful in his case against the Home Office.[17] The Court applied the principle of *Donoghue v Stevenson,* saying that the Borstal management should have foreseen that the boat seizure was likely to happen if venturesome boys escaped from their custody.

The reader should not gain the impression that a defence of statutory powers is easy to sustain but it is available and in a suitable case may be used successfully.

4 *The Limitation Acts.* The Limitation Act 1980 is the current consolidating Act. It sets out the time, starting with the date when a right to take legal action accrues, within which a person must begin his case at law. This rule is made so that there may be finality in litigation. Of course, any drawing of a line in respect of legal rights can cause hardship, so the Act endeavours to cater for that situation. The basic rules affecting a claim for damages for alleged negligence against a leisure services authority are accordingly:

1 The case must be brought within six years of the date when the right arose.
2 If personal injuries are involved, that period is reduced to three years.

3 Perhaps the plaintiff did not find out the cause of his damage as soon as he might have done because of fraud, mistake or concealment of facts. Then the limitation period, as it is called, runs from the date when he did find out 'or might with reasonable diligence have discovered it', to quote section 32 of the Act of 1980. Suppose an injury is caused in a gymnasium by a falling overhead bar. Suppose the ultimate cause was a rotted wooden beam in the underdrawing, to which the bar had been fastened. Suppose the entry of rain into that roof space was mentioned in a report to the building owners some years previously but that the presentation of that report and the nature of its recommendations did not become known to the plaintiff until more than three years after the accident. Then we might have the situation for which section 32 of the Act of 1980 was designed.

4 It should be borne in mind that there are special rules where the plaintiff suffers from mental illness, or is under 18 years or where the accident caused a death.

It is not popular to plead and rely for your defence on the Limitation Acts; but it is legal and it is done.

The Popplewell Report and The Green Guide[18]

These two documents are now required reading for managers of sports grounds.

The Green Guide is the Home Office Bible on ground layout, stand construction, the widths and numbers of entrances and exits and such relevant data. It is inevitable that any question of negligence by a manager will be looked at against the yardstick which the Green Guide furnishes. The Popplewell Report made 63 suggestions for altering the earlier edition of the Green Guide and the present edition takes account of those suggestions.

The Popplewell Report (referred to as 'Popplewell') made recommendations to amend the Safety of Sports Grounds Act 1975. So far as those are Acts or regulations or other positive law, we are not for the moment concerned to deal with them. But the issue of negligence was raised in the Bradford stadium case. It did not come into the reports but it gave rise to a public inquiry heard before Cantwell J, in which he apportioned blame between the Club and the inspecting local authority.

Legal lessons from Bradford football fire
It is desirable to try to record the lessons of that fire and subsequent legal action, for the benefit of leisure services managers, and these seem to be as follows:

1 If his property is within an Order under the Safety of Sports Grounds Act 1975, or the Fire Safety and Safety of Places of Sport Act 1987, he will have specific requirements to meet about fire precautions and other matters.

2 If not, he still has duties under the Occupiers Liability Acts 1957 and 1984. To lawful visitors, in particular, this is a high duty, discussed in Chapter 3.

3 Neither of these strict provisions ousts the Common Law duty in relation to negligence. This is residual and we have described its nature. The reason it remains, even after the above Act of 1957, is as follows. The Act of 1957 describes the occupiers' duty to visitors, ie the common duty of care, in terms

which do not fully extend to what have been called 'activity duties'. These are ones which would not have been encountered in a normal use of the premises. So if an unusual activity was under way at the sports ground, eg digging trenches for land drains, erecting a new electricity pylon in one corner, or putting up a big advertisement hoarding, it behoves leisure services managers to see that their visitors will not be exposed to a hazard on that account.

Conclusion

Negligence is not a very tidy tort. So although we have been trying to isolate a leisure service manager's legal liability for negligence in relation to staff situations, we have mentioned the circumstances when participants in games can give rise to claims, or, as in Popplewell, visitors at sporting events.

This is because managers and staff are both involved in seeing that these parties – both very welcome – come to no harm. However, if a mishap occurs, the legal relationship of manager and staff may come under the magnifying glass.

Notes

1 *Donoghue v Stevenson* (1932) AC 562.
2 *Bolam v Friern H.M.C.* (1957) 2 AER 118.
3 *Bourhill v Young* (1943) AC 92.
4 *Bolton v Stone* (1951) AC 580.
5 *Hilder v Associated Portland Cement Manufacturers Ltd* (1961) 3 AER 109.
6 *Fraser-Wallas v Waters & Waters* (1939) 4 AER 609.
7 *Murphy v Zoological Society of London* (1962) CLY 68.
8 *McKean v Raynor Bros. Ltd* (1942) 2 AER 650.
9 *Daniels v Whetstone Entertainments* (1962) 2 Lloyd's Rep.
10 *Lloyd v Grace-Smith* (1912) AC 716.
11 *Heasmans v Clarity Cleaning Co. Ltd* (1987) ICR 949.
12 *Latchford v Spedeworth International Ltd* (1984) 134 New LJ 36.
13 *Harrison v Vincent* (1982) RTR 8.
14 *Simms v Leigh R.F.C.* (1969) 2 AER 923.
15 *Murray v Harringay Arena Ltd* (1951) 2 AER 320.
16 *Haynes v Harwood* (1935) 1 KB 146.
17 *Home Office v Dorset Yacht Co.* (1970) AC 1004.
18 Committee of Inquiry into Crowd Safety and Control (the Popplewell Report Cmnd 9710 and the Guide to Safety at Sports Grounds – the Green Guide. Home Office. HMSO 1986).

4.2 Health and Safety Law – statutory provisions

The significance of the Health and Safety at Work Act 1974

This Act of 1974 was a landmark. For a century laws had been made to prescribe standards, first in factories, then in offices and shops. These were scattered, however, and a little ineffective. The Act of 1974 placarded the subject. It laid down universal standards, some for employers and some for employees. It created two new bodies to enforce these duties. It gave a public relations dimension to the whole subject. It linked enforcement with the new Industrial Tribunals, as well as the Magistrates Courts and, for appeals, with the higher Court system. Those earlier Acts about factories, shops and offices remain on the Statute Book but they were listed with many others in a Schedule of the Act of 1974 for codification in the course of time.[1] Their useful terms would thus be taken into one of the Codes of Practice, one of the other new features of this legislation.

We have mentioned the Act of 1974 but it must be emphasised that many of the requirements of that Act are embodied in regulations made under its powers. (The reader will find a fuller treatment of regulations as a form of law in Chapter 1.)

Health and Safety at Work Regulations

Regulations made under the Act can cover the following: allow exceptions generally from requirements or prohibitions, specify persons guilty of an offence, set out defences, restrict the punishment for particular offences, make requirements subject to approval by the Commission or other body and, lastly, make a specific authority responsible for enforcing certain statutory provisions (section 15). These are wide powers indeed.

Employer's duties

'It shall be the duty of every employer to ensure, so far as is reasonably practicable, the health safety and welfare at work of all his employees', the Act of 1974, section 2. This has the ring of the 11th Commandment about it. The Act then spells out those aspects of work to which the employer is called to give special attention.

These are plant and systems of work, arrangements for use, handling storage and transporting of 'articles and substances',[2] the provision of training about health and safety for his employees, keeping the place of work and its entrances safe and, finally, keeping the working environment safe and also adequate in relation to facilities for welfare at work.

The expression 'so far as is reasonably practicable' above, relates to all these items in the last paragraph. This has, not unnaturally, led to arguments, sometimes in Court, about whether a system provided fulfils this criterion. It seems clear in the first place, that the test is narrower than merely 'physically possible'. For instance the frequency of sweeping slippery substances from the floor in a food factory is one that can raise this question of 'reasonably practicable'. A lady who fell was found to have such smooth rubber soled shoes, against her employer's advice, that she failed in an action for recompense.[3] The number of sweepings per shift was accepted as reasonable.

The 'reasonably practicable' test also came under the judicial microscope in *Martin v Boulton & Paul (Steel Construction) Ltd* (1982).[4] A steel erector was fixing a girder without the precaution of a safety net, when he was struck by the crane sling and suffered injuries. The employers called evidence that they followed a practice which was almost universally accepted as reasonable. The Court was not happy that this approach complied with the test in the Act of 1974. To show a universal practice went some way, they said, but did not necessarily discharge the onus on the employer to show that it was not 'reasonably practicable' to use another, safer, method, under section 40 of this Act. This case demonstrates the high nature of the obligation placed upon employers.

A further duty of the employer is to publish a policy statement to demonstrate in public and particularly for the benefit of his employees, how he intends to discharge his duties under the Act.

He is to see that the health and safety of visitors and contractors is not at risk due to the state of the premises. This duty includes giving such visitors prescribed safety information. A tenant or contractor, in control of the premises under his tenancy or contract, is also placed under this duty. So a leisure services department, occupying as tenants land used as a sports field, would be at legal risk if visitors had to reach the site by crossing a bridge over a stream and there was a defective handrail on the bridge, about which no warning was given.

An employer is required to consult safety representatives of his employees about ways of achieving and maintaining the health and safety of the employees.[5] The parties are placed under a legal duty to cooperate in these matters.

Lastly, the employer, or other person in control, is to ensure that he uses the best practicable means to prevent noxious substances being emitted into the atmosphere. The exhaustive list of relevant processes in connection with this duty relates to industrial processes and so its relevance to the leisure services situation would seem to be minimal.

It should be noted that the employer is not at liberty to charge employees for any costs he incurs in relation to the above duties.

Employees' duties
These are gathered up into the omnibus duty to cooperate with the employer as he fulfils his various duties set out above.

An employee is also placed under a duty to take reasonable care for his own health and safety as well as for others who may be affected by his acts and omissions whilst at work.

In the leisure services situation of, for example, a swimming pool or sports centre, one could perhaps relate these duties to the temptation from time to time to by-pass agreed rules about the numbers and seniority of supervisors or attendants who will be in attendance at particular times.

General There is in the Act of 1974 a general prohibition on anyone intentionally or recklessly interfering with or misusing anything provided in connection with health, safety or welfare in pursuance of these provisions.

Such action could, in the ultimate, give rise to a criminal prosecution, eg for mischievously putting fire extinguishers out of action or possibly wilfully limiting ventilation provided in a salt or chemical store.

The Health and Safety Commission, the Codes of Practice and the Health and Safety Executive
The achievement of the purposes of the Act of 1974 is at Government level the responsibility of the Secretary of State for Employment. His two great aids are these newly created bodies the Health and Safety Commission and the Health and Safety Executive. The Commission is charged with handling strategy, whilst the Executive deals with the tactics, the day to day problems, particularly enforcement.

The Commission   The Commission's general duty is to further the purposes of the Act as set out in section 1, namely:

1 Secure the health, safety and welfare of people at work.
2 Protect other persons against risks to their health and safety from people at work.
3 Control dangerous substances.
4 Control emission into the atmosphere of offensive substances.

Duties 3 and 4 will affect few of the activities of those engaged in the leisure services; duties 1 and 2 affect everyone.

With this remit, the Commission are empowered to carry out research and update Government and other relevant bodies of their findings, to keep abreast of subjects within their remit by specialist Advisory Committees and these may include one about nuclear safety.

Codes of Guidance   When a particular area of activity justifies the step, the Commission may promulgate a Code of Practice. This is a legally created document, made only after consultation with the Secretary of State.[6] Breach of its terms is regarded as a breach of duty and like that more familiar Code, the Highway Code, it may be referred to in legal proceedings for a specific offence under the Act of 1974. The Code provides public evidence that a standard in a particular area of activity was known to a defendant who, presumably, chose to do something which departed from that standard. Like the Highway Code also, these Codes of Practice are to be kept up to date with amendments which take account of changes in knowledge.

The Commission is also the body which is designated in the Consumer Protection Act 1987 (section 11) for consultation by the Secretary of State for Trade and Industry, when Regulations are to be made about 'goods suitable for use at work'.

Finally, Guidance Notes, whilst having no legal force, may be issued by both Commission and Executive to give interested parties practical advice on problems they may encounter in this vast field.

Attention is drawn to published documents, in final form, on the subject of Safety in Fairgrounds and, in draft form, Safety in Swimming Pools. These are a little short of the authority of Codes of Guidance yet they are issued under the aegis of the Health and Safety Executive (HSE). It is the National

Industry Group for Local Government of the Health and Safety Executive which produced the swimming pool document above in 1986. A most comprehensive document, variously referred to as a directive and a guidance leaflet, it is clearly capable of being referred to in prosecutions as promulgating a standard which the HSE consider suitable for the particular field of activity.

The Executive As the sharp end of Government arrangements, the Executive, with three members, controls the Health and Safety inspectorate and the 21 area offices, each under a director, which operate to enforce the Act of 1974.

They may obtain information, carry out inspections and issue Improvement and Prohibition Notices. The first gives legal impetus to get some work done, the second is to stop imminent dangers. Recipients can appeal against these notices to Industrial Tribunals.[7] For example a company owned 31 betting shops and was served with an Improvement Notice due to failure to issue any Policy Statement, as required by the Act of 1974, about its health and safety practices. As each premise had less than five employees, the defendants argued that they were exempt from the Act. They did not succeed with this contention, the High Court, on appeal, holding that the 31 shops could comprise one 'undertaking', the word used in the Act. The case was remitted to magistrates to settle this point after evidence on the facts about the extent of central control to which each shop was subject.[8]

Unlawful discrimination Readers may note that the Equal Opportunities Commission, constituted under the Sex Discrimination Act 1975, Part VI, has an inspectoral role to keep under review the operation of these Health and Safety Act provisions for any that show discrimination between men and women. They draw the attention of the Secretary of State to any such practices.

Offences
The Act of 1974 creates a large number of offences, most carrying a fine of £1000 or more, some also bearing the sanction of imprisonment. Among those of great relevance to leisure service employers we may mention:

1 Acting without a licence.
2 Failing to discharge any of the general duties.
3 Intentionally making a false statement in an official register or other book.
4 Contravening Improvement or Prohibition Notices.

In conclusion, since the Act of 1974 carries 53 sections, it will be apparent that the outline given here is made with the leisure service reader in mind and cannot claim to be all-embracing.

The Offices Shops and Railway Premises Act 1963

If the Health and Safety at Work Act 1974 provides the main, overarching, law about health, safety and welfare at work, this older, still existing, law should be known so far at least as it touches on standards in offices. It may also affect leisure service managers if they look after a shop. If they should also happen to be associated with a light railway, they might cast an eye over the third part of this Act of 1963. The main feature of its provisions is its practical nature.

The premises must be clean. For work where physical effort is not involved, working temperature below 60.8°F after the first hour is not acceptable. The premises must not be overcrowded. They must be adequately lit and ventilated. Sufficient sanitary appliances must be provided. Washing facilities and drinking water must be provided. So must accommodation for clothing. Eating facilities for employees who eat meals at work and seats for employees are two further stipulations in this Act. Finally, steps, stairs, floors and passages are to be safe.

An employer, faced with prosecution, may escape punishment if he can satisfy the Court that he acted with due diligence to comply. Employees are to have accessible, eg on a staff notice board, a copy of the Abstract of the Act and the Regulations made under it.

Employer's Liability (Compulsory Insurance) Act 1969

Though this Act does not apply to local authorities, it does apply to, for example, private sports clubs and is thus worth inclusion.

It requires every employer to take out insurance of not less than £2m against liability for bodily injury and disease, sustained by his employees, arising out of their employment.

It is supported by a penalty for conviction for failure so to insure, of a maximum of £500 per day and other penalties for not meeting the requirements of inspectors from the Health and Safety Executive or not displaying their insurance certificate.

Fire Precautions Act 1971 as amended by the Fire Safety and Safety of Places of Sport Act 1987

Local fire authorities are responsible for enforcing the relevant provisions of these Acts and associated Regulations. Whilst there are lists of features in buildings which are the focus of interest for fire authorities, it is possible to itemise the general scheme of the law so that leisure service managers can appreciate how the premises for which they have responsibility fit into that scheme:

Cinemas
These remain within the provisions of the Manufacture of Film Regulations 1928 and the Cinematograph Film Stripping Regulations 1939. These cover the precautions needed in rooms where such film is stored, repaired or used. Certificates and the sanction of fines are part of the enforcement procedures employed in the Regulations.

Workplaces
When workplaces are used by more than twenty people at one time, and

more than ten work elsewhere than on the ground floor, then, without going into fine detail, the premises would seem likely to require a Fire Certificate.

Such a certificate will specify: the use of the premises; its means of escape and the effective ways to use those means; its fire fighting equipment; and the ways in which fire warnings are given on the premises.

Some premises were certified before 1 January 1971, ie when the Act of 1971 took effect. They remain under those certificates. More recent buildings require certificates under the Act of 1971.

The fire authority is primarily concerned about the four matters mentioned above, and will need an application and accompanying plans of the building in order to determine the specific requirements to be imposed.

Even if the premises should fall below the qualifying standard for full fire certificates, they come within the Act of 1971 for what are called non-certificated premises. These cover outward opening doors, the marking of exits, the enclosure of hoists, and lift ways, in order to give a 30 minute protective fire resistance period from the enclosing materials.

Again in all office and shop premises, there must be free passage through a workroom, means for fighting fires available for use and unlocked doors so that easy egress is possible.

The legal framework thus described is comprehensive in relation to offices and shops and workplaces.

Changes made by the Act of 1987

The Act of 1987 was enacted after the Popplewell Report and proceeds by amendments to the Act of 1971. Doubtless these will be consolidated when there is time. For the moment we summarise the changes:

1 Exemption from the need for a fire certificate for premises may be granted but can be accompanied by specifying the number of persons who can safely be in the premises at one time. Recent inspection is a condition of this grant of exemption. Exemptions may be withdrawn in the light of fire risks and in accordance with a procedure which affords to the occupier of the premises an opportunity to make representations before a decision is made (section 1).
2 Charges may be made for fire certificates.
3 Even though exempt from the need for a full fire certificate, the premises may need to comply with requirements for means of escape in case of fire and about fire fighting equipment.
4 Codes of Practice can be issued; their legal effect will be similar to other Codes described earlier.
5 Following a specific recommendation in Popplewell, improvement notices can be issued, to have the similar immediate effect as those under the Health and Safety at Work Act. The concentration is on fire fighting equipment and means of escape.
6 Generally wider powers are granted to fire authorities and there is a tightening up of the law.

Offences are created by the Act of 1971 ranging from a maximum fine of £1000 for failure to comply with the terms of a Fire Certificate to £30 for not keeping a copy of the Fire Certificate at the premises. Powers of appeal against decisions of a local fire authority exist.

The pattern of these Acts of 1971 and 1987 is to allow the fire authorities to keep abreast of relevant changes in the use or layout of the leisure service premises, the inadequacy of fire fighting equipment and other relevant features in their enforcement policy. Their power of inspection is important and is used extensively.

Notes

1 There are 31 of these Acts. The procedure was novel and interesting.
2 Not defined. A classic case under another Act once decided that 'article' included a goldfish.
3 *Braham v J. Lyons & Co Ltd* (1962) 3 AER 281.
4 *Martin v Boulton & Paul (Steel Construction) Ltd* (1982) ICR 366.
5 Election to a Safety Committee is in accordance with the Safety Representatives and Safety Committees Regulations 1977 (SI 1977 No 500).
6 Act of 1974 section 16.
7 Act of 1974 section 24.
8 *Osborne v Bill Taylor of Huyton Ltd* (1982) ICR 168.

4.3 Employment law

Engaging staff. The contract of employment

Within 13 weeks of an employee starting to work for him, an employer is required to give the employee a statement about the terms on which he is employed. It is possible to get a pro forma for this statement which must list:

1 The title of the job.
2 The details of remuneration.
3 The date when employment starts.
4 The period of notice needed to terminate it.
5 Details about any pension and sickness schemes relevant to the job.
6 Particulars of grievance and disciplinary procedures.[1]
7 A statement about whether the last employment of the new employee is to count as 'continuous employment' with the new work the employee has begun. This is because 'continuous employment' is important in the Employment Protection (Consolidation) Act 1978 in establishing various legal rights.[2]

It would sometimes be sensible to delay handing over the statement until the end of the thirteen week statutory period, in case the employee proved to be a short stayer.

Dismissing staff. General

An employer may wish to dismiss an employee for good reason and, provided this is done lawfully, it should be upheld both in the Courts and the Industrial Tribunals.

Summarily
Instant or summary dismissal is usually the subject of a term in the general conditions of employment of employees. It has to be brought into individual contracts of employment by some clear provision to that effect. Theft, fighting, violence at work, insubordination, would be the sort of items an employer might wish to list in the contract so that he could deal with them in that way.

The term 'gross misconduct' is sometimes used in such a contract, to show that it is an extreme solution for extreme misconduct.

The Courts do not like the term, thinking it almost indefinable in the abstract. What it means is that extreme misconduct, in relation to that particular job, which the employer has selected as being so unacceptable that he cannot tolerate a culpable employee working his notice. He must depart forthwith.

So the Court agreed that instant dismissal was justified, when an inspector of croupiers was summarily dismissed after a croupier was found by him to be cheating and he deliberately overlooked the matter.[3]

Again, a drinks waiter who defrauded customers not only by overcharging them but also by charging them twice – once individually and once as members of a party – was rightly summarily dismissed, said the Court.[4]

On the other hand, a summary dismissal was not upheld when an aggrieved employee called her employer 'a bastard'. She was in a car on her way home with another employee, who reported the conversation to the employer.[5]

There is no shortage of examples for guidance on the merits of a summary dismissal.

By notice

We turn to the more usual way in which employees are dismissed. The above Act of 1978 stipulates the length of notice appropriate for employees in relation to their period of service. We emphasise that this is when the ground for dismissal is not of the sort dealt with above.

The periods are:

Employment less than 2 years – notice not less than 1 week.
Employment 2 years or more but less than 12 – 1 week for each year.
Employment 12 years or more – not less than 12 weeks' notice.[6]

An employee of at least 6 months' standing can legally ask for a statement of the reasons for his dismissal. This is to be supplied within 14 days of the request.[7]

Unfair dismissals

In the last 30 years the law has developed rapidly to allow a challenge before industrial tribunals for unfair dismissals. This is a complex subject and we limit this outline to the basic features likely to be met in leisure service management situations.

The law begins by conferring a right on every employee 'not to be unfairly dismissed'.[8]

Many dismissals which give rise to applications to industrial tribunals are due to the inadequate way in which the employee performs his job ('capability') or to his misconduct while at work ('conduct') or his lack of some qualifications, eg a heavy goods vehicle licence, to be able to carry out his job within the law ('duty or restriction imposed by an enactment') or perhaps a management decision to delete his post from the establishment and payroll ('redundancy'). There is a fifth group – 'some other substantial reason' – which is often related to a business reason of the employer. For instance, he may need to alter the conditions of work or the hours or some other terms because of a change in the nature of the business. By way of a completely different example and to emphasise the wide range of this fifth group, if a husband and wife team are wardens or caretakers at a holiday camp and, say, the husband is dismissed for misconduct, then it has been held to be 'practical' that the wife should also be dismissed.[9] This is an instance where neither capability nor conduct nor redundancy nor statutory reason are involved. It becomes 'some other substantial reason' within section 57 of the Act of 1978 and an acceptable dismissal in the tribunal's view under that Act.

In these cases it is for the employer to satisfy a tribunal about the reason for the dismissal and if it is one of these five cases, the tribunal has to decide if the dismissal was 'fair'. In doing this the tribunal are to take account of the size of the employer's business. They are then to look at the dismissal from the point of view of an employer in that style of business and determine whether the dismissal was within what has been called the range of responses of a reasonable employer.[10]

Their decision has to be reached 'in accordance with equity and the substantial merits of the case'. This approach has encouraged Appeal Courts to trust the tribunals as the main arbiters of these cases. This means that those Courts discourage the creation of a system of binding precedents such as applies in some branches of the law. Intervention and upsetting a tribunal's decision is accordingly limited to those extreme cases where it seems that the tribunal has misdirected itself on the law or has come to a conclusion that no reasonable tribunal could have reached (ie the decision was 'perverse').

A successful claimant in an action for unfair dismissal may achieve reinstatement or re-engagement, on the one hand, or alternatively, compensation. The first is a return to the same job as before dismissal. The second is a return to another job with the same employer. The third is a sum of money calculated as specified in the Act of 1978.

This consists of first a basic amount related to the age, wage and length of service of the claimant. To this is added, secondly, a compensatory amount. This is designed to allow for past and future losses resulting from the dismissal. It takes account of his own conduct in so far as it may have contributed to the dismissal; it also allows for the future difficulty of regaining the same income he enjoyed under the last job.[11] It is a comprehensive amount that can take account of loss of car and pension rights, holiday club benefits or travel allowances. The Act contains a maximum stopper on the compensation thus calculated.[12]

If the question of compensation should arise when the parties are in negotiation, it is as well to have these statutory guidelines in mind. In a case about the Chelsea Football Club, a payment of £7500 was agreed and made to a talent scout, who a new manager decided was not of any great advantage to the club. It took a case in the Courts to sort out this money and make it accord with the dismissed employee's legal rights, as this aspect had not been taken into account originally.[13]

Valid and invalid dismissals

It seemed desirable to describe first the general framework of dismissal law, relating to notices, valid reasons, compensation and the basis of industrial tribunal decisions. We did this since, in practice, those elements occur in a large proportion of the cases that come before industrial tribunals.

Against that background, we can now deal a little more briefly with some of the special cases dealt with in the Employment Acts. These concern trade union activities, redundancy and pregnancy. After that, we shall turn to the exceptions from these procedures.

It is nonetheless worth emphasising that many possible cases en route to industrial tribunals as 'unfair dismissals' simply stop after a first question from a solicitor reveals that the employee had less than two years' employment before the dismissal. The qualifying period is essential if these rights are to be exercised.[14]

Trade union activities

Unfair dismissals   We have discussed above the sort of matters a tribunal has to weigh up when deciding if a dismissal was fair or unfair, within the Employment Act criteria. The balance can be quite a delicate one at times. In the case of trade union activities, however, Parliament has removed some of those areas for debate. The Employment Acts of 1978 and 1982 now make a dismissal unfair if it was carried out because:

1 the employee was or proposed to become a member of an independent trade union; or
2 the employee had taken or proposed to take part at any appropriate time in the activities of an independent trade union; or
3 the employee was not a member of any trade union.

These are three separate reasons and as they are accompanied in the Acts by careful definitions and some qualifications, the reader must refer to the Acts themselves if he comes across one these situations.[15]

Fair dismissals   However a dismissal can be legally fair, for non-membership of a specified independent trade union. This however only happens when three important conditions are fulfilled. These are:

1 it is the practice, at the establishment in question, to join a specified independent trade union; and also,
2 a principal or substantial reason for the dismissal is that the employee was not a member of that trade union; and also,
3 the closed shop had the status of having been approved by a postal ballot, complying with the Act and held within five years of the dismissal. (The Act then sets out the various percentages for the ballot in question to meet this condition.)

If however any of the following five conditions is met, the above 'fair dismissal' does not apply. These are:

1 the employee was a non-trade union member for the stated five year period; or
2 the employee objects on genuine conscientious grounds to joining a trade union; or
3 the employee participated in the ballot by which the closed shop agreement at this establishment came into existence after 14 August 1980 and has not been a member of a trade union since that time; or
4 an employee's declaration of unreasonable expulsion from a trade union existed or was the subject of proceedings before an industrial tribunal at the time of the dismissal; or
5 the employee's refusal to take part in a strike (giving rise to his expulsion) or to join a trade union was due to the terms of a written code of conduct for employees of his qualifications and 2 and 4 above do not apply.

This is admittedly complex but it is hoped that the outline given will alert leisure service managers to the considerations that will arise when they meet this sort of situation.

Redundancy
We shall deal now shortly with the law about unfair dismissal in relation to a redundancy situation. Before doing so, it is worth taking note of the fact that redundancy will be met by leisure service managers in two other possible situations.

First, they may have to make for example a team trainer redundant and have to make a redundancy payment to him. He is entitled to this if he is an employee with at least two years' service, who has been dismissed on the above ground. The payment is based on a graduated scale and depends on his age, wage and length of service.[16]

Secondly, when a business, in our case say a sports club or centre or similar leisure service business, is transferred to a new owner, it may be that not all employees are also transferred. Some may be made redundant. The obligation to make redundancy payments will fall on one of the two owners. This is a complex area of law.[17]

Normal case of redundancy dismissal   We turn then to the case of unfair dismissal claims based upon redundancy. The employer has to be ready to meet challenges which will usually allege one of the following:

That he failed to warn adequately that redundancy was pending.
That he failed to make his selection for redundancy fairly, in relation to the group of employees to which he limited the selection (this raises both the criteria of selection he said he would use and the basis of selection he did in fact use).
That he failed to consult the dismissed employee in a meaningful way.
That he failed to consider alternative employment, possibly on reduced hours, which could be offered to the employee, before he resorted to dismissal.

The cases show that these are all possible areas for argument before a tribunal in relation to a general contention that a dismissal for redundancy was unfair.
What we must stress however, is that none of the points above has to be met by the employer as a legal condition to make a dismissal 'fair'. A tribunal looks at the total situation to see if an employer followed a fair system.[18] Size of business is very important. The absence of a personnel officer can indicate that a breezy sorting out of problems was normal. Again, the number of employees being made redundant is important. The other important points for a tribunal are the existence of a trade union and the existence of any document setting our grievance and disciplinary procedures. Moreover a tribunal's decision might be upset on appeal, if it did not consider whether the decision to dismiss fell within the range of possible responses of a reasonable employer in that line of business.

Usually about half of cases begun are settled between the parties before they reach the tribunal; the ones that do arrive are those where the parties think that some of the points mentioned above are arguable.

Unfair dismissal for redundancy   There is a special case where the Employment Acts specify a dismissal for redundancy as unfair. This is where:

1 he has not dismissed other employees who were in the same position as

the dismissed employee, in relation to both the redundancy situation and the jobs they did; and
2 either the real reason related to trade union activities or, in selecting the particular employee, the employer was departing from an agreed procedure within that undertaking.[19]

The employer forced into this legal corner can only escape by showing one of four things:

1 The employee, if retained, would have been in breach of some enactment.
2 There was 'some other substantial reason' for the dismissal, eg conflict of personalities.
3 He was a temporary replacement for a permanent employee: he knew this when engaged and the permanent employee is now back at work.
4 Similarly, she was engaged as a temporary stand-in for a pregnant employee, who has now returned. Again, she knew this when she was accepted for the position.

Pregnancy
A dismissal is, by statute, unfair, unless:

1 at the time in question, the employee will, by reason of her pregnancy, have become unable to do her work adequately; or
2 some statutory provision would be contravened if she continued working.

An employer has limited options to counter this role of unfairness in the circumstances set out. He is put under an onus to show that he is offering the lady a new and equivalent job, with certain refinements which must be studied for the detail.[20]

Exceptions

There are eight exceptions to these general rights of complaint to industrial tribunals for unfair dismissal. They are all special cases, viz

1 Dockworkers.
2 Persons working in fishing vessels on a non-sharing basis.
3 Persons whose contracts of employment involve their normally working outside the UK.
4 Persons working on ships which are registered in Great Britain but whose employment is normally outside Britain or who are not normally resident in this country.
5 An employee who, when the notice expires, has reached his normal retiring age.
6 Employees who have not sufficient length of employment to qualify to apply to a tribunal, currently two years.
7 If there is no prescribed retiring age, that he has reached pensionable age.
8 Persons employed by their husbands or wives.

General

It may surprise readers to know, in the light of the above, that in a recent case, support was given by the President of the Employment Appeal Tribunal to the view that, in employment law, Parliament intended to 'banish legalism'.

Industrial tribunals, said Waite J, should not 'subject the authorities to the same analysis as a court of law searching in a plethora of precedent for binding or persuasive authority'.[21]

Within the chosen limits of this work, we do not touch on the rare cases that raise principles of national security nor dismissals under pressure of strikes or lock outs. Both are touched on in the Employment Acts.

Ongoing legal obligations of employers and employees

We close this section by mentioning a number of conditions which are deemed to be within contracts of employment or which merit careful thought before being so included. Their common element is that it is the common law which provides the legal background, rather than statutes.

Mutual trust and confidence

'It is clearly established that there is implied in a contract of employment a term that the employers will not, without reasonable and proper cause, conduct themselves in a manner calculated or likely to destroy or seriously damage the relationship of confidence and trust between employer and employee.'[22] This is an important statement of a well established principle in employment law. It may be thought to be stating the obvious but it is sometimes reassuring to find that the law actually does this!

So, where an employer said to his employee, 'You can't do the b . . . job anyway,' and said it maliciously, to get rid of him, the Courts found that the employee had a reasonable case of unfair constructive dismissal – in ordinary parlance, he could say that he felt forced to resign.[23] This condition carries implications for both parties – it is about 'mutual' trust and confidence.

On the employee's side, the term is critical in relation to the employer's trade secrets. A recent authoritative case[24] has listed three groups of these secrets:

1 Information, which, because anyone could find it, is not exclusive employer's information and therefore not protected.
2 Information the employer has said is confidential or by its nature is so. This is a trade secret as long as the employment continues.
3 A trade secret stipulated to last for ever, such as proprietary formulae or processes.

On these, it has been laid down that the position of the employee in the business is critical, as is the nature of the alleged secret. So simple addresses or telephone numbers of customers would not seem to be secret within this principle. The other critical factors are how far the employer imposed the confidentiality upon the employee and how far it is possible to separate the allegedly secret information from disclosable information.

This whole area of law may well be relevant to managers of sports centres or theatres, who can negotiate favourable discounts from artistes or sportsmen on account of continuing contracts. It clearly behoves such managers to pay attention to the limited protection some 'trade secrets' are now given in the Courts.

Competence
An employee is liable for his own negligence during his work, eg to another employee or a customer.

For his part the employer is to provide competent foremen, reliable plant and a safe system of work. The 'drop' scene in 'Maria Martin and the Red Barn' provides a classical example of this principle.[25] The villain in this melodrama was to be executed by hanging. The stage manager successfully demonstrated how to fall onto the mattress behind the scenery, but when the actor did it he broke his ankle. He sued, saying the mattress wasn't thick enough nor was the system safe. He lost, at the level of the Court of Appeal. The employer does not *guarantee* the actor's safety; he is to use reasonable care to see that his plant and systems are safe and in this case the defendant satisfied the Court that he had done so.

European Community
We are now part of the European Community (EC) and their law is our law. Readers will know of the pressure which this country has come under in relation to the age of retirement for men and women, due to EC decisions. Some of our employment law has been specifically enacted in order to comply with those decisions. We cannot enter upon that subject now, other than to give a warning about its relevance, and quote Lord Denning's well-known words 'In future in transactions which cross the frontier, we must no longer think of English law as something on its own. We must speak and think of Community law, of Community rights and obligations and we must give effect to them. We have to learn a new system. We must get down to it.'[26]

Notes

1 The Employment Protection (Consolidation) Act 1978 section 1 consolidated statutes about employment from 1963 onwards. It is still the main source of this branch of law.
2 It is guaranteed under schedule 13 paras 17–18 of the Act when the last and the new employer have the right degree of legal association.
3 *Turner v Pleasurama Casinos Ltd* (1976) 1 RLR 151.
4 *T H F Leisure Ltd v Aquilar* (1976) 1 RLR 251.
5 *Ismond v Nelson Coin Automatics Ltd* (1975) 1 RLR 173.
6 Section 49 of the Act of 1978.
7 Section 53. A defaulting employer may have to pay a sum equal to two weeks' pay.
8 Section 54. None of this discussion is to suggest that a common law right of action for 'wrongful dismissal' is impaired. Far from it. The point is that the claim for unfair dismissal before an industrial tribunal is the practical right available and used in ninety per cent of cases leisure service managers are likely to meet.
9 *Kelman v Oram* (1983) 1 RLR 432.
10 Section 57 and *Rolls-Royce Ltd v Walpole* (1980) 1 RLR 343.
11 Sections 72–76A.
12 At present £8500, Act of 1978 section 75.
13 *Chelsea F.C. and Athletic Co. v Heath* (1981) ICR 323.

14 Section 64.
15 Act of 1978 section 58.
16 He must be over 18 and work 16 hours a week or have five years' service if he only works 8 to 16 hours a week. It is assumed also that the employee has not been offered another job nor dismissed summarily. *See* Part IV of Act of 1978.
17 See especially section 94 of Act of 1978. The existence and nature of the redundancy fund, on which some payments of redundancy monies may fall, is described in sections 103–109 of the Act of 1978.
18 See especially *Williams and others v Compair Maxam Ltd* (1982) ICR 156, but also the line of cases modifying and explaining that decision, leading currently to *Polkey v A. E. Dayton Services Ltd* (1987) ICR 301.
19 Act of 1978 section 59.
20 Act of 1978 section 60. *Grimsby Carpet Co. Ltd v Bedford* (1987) ICR 975 shows pregnancy discussed in relation to unfair dismissal generally.
21 *Amandarajah v Lord Chancellor's Dept* (1984) 1 RLR 131.
22 *Woods v W. M. Car Services (Peterborough) Ltd* (1981) per Browne-Wilkinson J ICR 666.
23 *Courtaulds Northern Textiles v Andrew* (1979) 1 RLR 84.
24 *Faccenda Chicken Ltd v Fowler* (1986) ICR 297.
25 *Fanton v Denville* (1932) 2 KB 309.
26 *Bulmer v Bollinger SA and others* (1974) AER 1226.

4.4 Discrimination

a Sex discrimination

Equal pay
The Equal Pay Act 1970 as amended provides for an individual to be treated not less favourably than a person of the opposite sex who works for the same employer. This legal right is to apply where:

1 the two persons are employed on like work (ie the same work or work which is broadly similar);
2 they are on work which has been rated as equivalent under a job evaluation scheme; or
3 they are on work which is of equal value.

This equal treatment is with regard to pay and the other terms of the contract of employment.

This Act is accordingly about *matters within the work situation*. We shall consider first the general legal provisions, then some examples of its operation and then the defences available to employers when cases are brought against them.

General legal position under the Act of 1970 An equality clause is deemed to be contained in every contract of employment, where a woman is employed at an 'establishment' in Great Britain. This means that the existing terms are deemed modified so that they are no less favourable to a woman than to a man, doing 'like work'. Though the Act's wording suggests that women will be the sex who complain of unfair discrimination, it applies to men as well and one or two cases over the years have shown that this Act can work 'in both directions', as Lord Denning once put it.[1]

It is not always easy to find a man doing 'like work' but that is what the woman who wishes to assert her rights under this Act has to do before she takes her case to an industrial tribunal. The man is called the comparator. Suppose that no men are working as typists or secretaries in a firm where a group of typists consider that they are being discriminated against on account of their sex. They may now pursue their case based on some employee doing work of 'like value', rather than like work.[2] One of the first successful cases brought under this provision was brought by a canteen assistant who put up a painter as a man doing work of like value.

It was the European Community (EC) which, in the Treaty of Rome, laid down the broad principle of equal pay for equal work to which the British Act of 1970 was a response. Likewise the British 1983 Regulations about 'equal value' were this country's response to certain EC regulations and a case heard before the European Court of Justice.

Examples It is not easy to find a case specifically related to the field of leisure services.

There are however a number of cases about jobs which occur freely in that area as well as in other fields and thus may be of interest. Thus women cleaners have succeeded under this Act of 1970 in showing discrimination in their wages compared with men cleaners. Another case concerned a vending machine assistant and a third concerned a woman driver. In one case, a woman sales clerk was successful in showing that her wages were less than for a man doing the same job. The case argued in Court was that the man's wage was enhanced because he was engaged on the same wage that he had with his last employer. The applicant had a strong case; she had trained the man to do the job, she drew £5 a week less in wages and she had three years' greater experience at the work than him. In deciding in her favour, the Court of Appeal said that the item about the man's last job was simply 'an extrinsic circumstance'; they did not think it constituted 'a material difference not based on sex', which is what the Act requires before different pay for the same work can be accepted.[3]

Employers' defences These perhaps involve the point mentioned in the last example. When seeking to justify different pay for equal work an employer may adduce economic reasons, business grounds, perhaps experience. The defence is not an easy one to establish. He has to expect searching examination by the Court on whether the material difference was the genuine cause of the pay differential.

Equal Opportunities Commission At the back of this branch of the law – and sometimes in front! – is the Equal Opportunities Commission. This was set up in the Sex Discrimination Act 1975 and is responsible for working towards the 'elimination of discrimination' and also 'providing equality of opportunity between men and women generally'.[4] It is this wide remit which has led the Commission to be involved in some of the notable test cases on this law before the European Court of Justice during recent years.

Sex discrimination
Discrimination on the grounds of sex which takes place within the working day is what we have been considering so far. When we turn to discrimination of that nature which occurs outside that field, we reach the subject matter of the Sex Discrimination Act 1975. The subject matter is large, for it includes education, employment, advertising, the provision of goods or services or facilities and also the disposal or managing of premises.

It will perhaps not surprise the reader to learn that this Act of 1975 has 86 sections and a number of schedules. It thus becomes necessary to select those areas of law of special interest to leisure services managers. In doing so, we shall omit educational establishments and a number of special cases, as mineworkers, ministers of religion, police and prison officers.

The pattern of the Act of 1975 is first to set out the general principle, which is to apply to stated areas of our social life. Excepted areas are then specified. The Act proceeds to set up the Equal Opportunities Commission, which we have just referred to. It also describes the role of industrial tribunals in the enforcement of offences created by the Act and lastly, other ways in which the Act is enforced. It will be recalled that the European Court of Justice has jurisdiction in the whole field and cannot be ignored when the aspect of enforcement is considered. Our topics will accordingly be: general principles; the employment field; other areas and activities; exceptions; and enforcement.

General principles Direct sex discrimination occurs when a person of one sex is treated less favourably on the ground of sex than a person of the other sex would be in the same or not materially different circumstances.[5]

The scheme of the Act of 1975 is to describe later a number of situations where that form of discrimination is unlawful and thereby constitutes an offence.

Thus, when a woman was refused service at the bar of El Vino's in 1983 and made to sit at a table for waiter service, she successfully made out a case of unlawful discrimination under this Act. The Court of Appeal said that the Act was a simple one, seeking to deal with ordinary everyday behaviour and the relative positions of men and women. They discouraged a technical approach.[6]

Employment field – genuine occupational qualifications The Act continues by bringing within its definition discrimination which uses more subtle means. The simple example is the advert for men and women to apply for a job but which then imposes a condition which, in practice, excludes women. The Act refers to such a condition as one 'to her detriment'.[7] The Act is sexually neutral, so that men as well as women are protected against unlawful discrimination. This obliges the framers of the Act to state that any preference shown to women in connection with pregnancy or childbirth is to be ignored for the purposes of the Act.

We cannot pretend that the existence of unlawful sex discrimination is always easy to determine. For instance, it is not unlawful to treat men and women differently when the primary reason is difference of training or experience or perhaps on commercial grounds. On the other hand, an employer's good intention cannot avoid the proscribed conduct. So a nursery gardener fell foul of the Act by declining an application for a vacancy by 'a young mum with two kiddies', on the ground that she would be failing her domestic duties. Again a cinema broke the law as laid down in this Act by declining an application for usherette from a man. Again, it was unlawful to dismiss a van driver because he refused an order to remove a stud earring, it coming to light that two of the same company's women drivers were allowed to wear earrings at work. Examples can be found also in the field of dress. An employer required a woman employee to wear overalls against her wishes, yet men doing the same job were allowed to wear lounge suits. A woman who wore trousers at work was dismissed. On complaining, the tribunal said the dress requirement was not of sufficient import to be to the lady's 'detriment', within the Act (*Schmidt v Austicks Bookshops Ltd* 1978).

However there are jobs where the employer's choice of the sex for the job is recognised as reasonable. This is a group of jobs which is taken out of the Act of 1975.

1 Where the nature of the job calls for a man on the ground of stamina, physiology or strength or in the interests of authenticity in drama.

2 Where the choice of one sex only is in the interests of privacy or decency, eg bath or sauna attendants, so that one sex cannot object on account of the job being done by someone of the other sex.

3 Where the nature or location of the job obliges the employers to provide

sleeping accommodation and sanitary conveniences and it would be unreasonable to expect him to do so for both sexes, in order to have privacy in their use of those facilities.

4 Where there are personal services to be performed and these are best carried out by one sex.

5 Where it is necessary to meet legal requirements.

6 Where the nature of the job requires it to be carried out by a married couple.[8]

Other areas For examples of unlawful discrimination see the following list, all of which would seem feasible in the leisure services field:

1 Refusing to provide for a woman, or deliberately omitting to provide to the same standard as for a man, goods, facilities or services available for the public. This could be access to a sports stand or part of an entertainment centre, such as a theatre or cinema.

2 When disposing of or managing property eg letting the franchise for an ice cream kiosk.

3 Discriminating in the course of work by a contract worker.

4 Publishing advertisements which indicate an intention to carry out an unlawful act of discrimination.

5 Instructing another person to do an unlawful act or putting pressure on him to do so.

Exceptions *Training bodies* Where training is given to one sex only, that might be, within the definitions of this Act, a service of a discriminatory nature. However it is exempted from that risk if, in the preceding 12 months, there were no members of one sex in Great Britain engaged in that work, or the numbers of that sex so engaged were comparatively small, and it takes the right legal steps to meet the situation. This the Act describes as positive action and approval from the Secretary of State is needed for a training body to be authorised to offer this training to encourage members of the sex in question to take up such activity. Section 47 in the Act of 1975 contains the procedure for handing this special situation.

Sport There is also a general exception for acts relating to participation as a competitor in certain sporting events which are confied to one sex. The sports to which the exception applies are those in which physical strength, stamina or physique are important, so that the average woman would be at a disadvantage in competition with the average man.[9]

Enforcement This may involve action by way of a complaint by an individual. He can go to an industrial tribunal, if the discrimination was in relation to employment. That tribunal can order payment of compensation by the offending party, recommend action to rectify the damage caused and also declare the rights of the parties.[10]

When the subject matter is not an employment situation, it goes to the County Court. This deals with the claim like one in a Court for civil wrong, making declarations, awarding damages, granting injunctions, making orders and otherwise as appropriate. Damages can include an item for injured feelings.

The other main avenue for enforcement rests with the Equal Opportunities Commission:

1 In respect of unlawful acts of discrimination, the Commission may issue a Non-Discrimination Notice calling on the recipient to desist and take other steps as detailed.
2 Before doing this, the Commission advise the offender that such a notice is possible and invite his representations first.
3 If such a notice is issued, the recipient can appeal to an industrial tribunal or to the County Court, depending upon the subject matter, as mentioned above. They have the powers listed above.

Further, the Commission can conduct what the Act calls investigations. These would be for an individual offence as a preliminary to the issue of notices dealt with above. Alternatively they could be for a major malpractice in industry or commerce. The Commission has wide powers of securing information in this situation. They act under the Secretary of State for Employment and report to him also.

Lastly the Act provides a procedure to secure amendment of any contract which contains a discriminatory clause in terms contravening some provision in the Act of 1975. This is where the victim of the discrimination is a party to the contract in question. (If he is not, the clause is simply void and unenforceable.) He can go to the County Court (or Sheriff Court in Scotland) which may then remove or modify the offending clause.[11]

Code of Practice   The Equal Opportunities Commission has published a Code of Practice which sets out the standards they wish to see followed by all those subject to this Act.[12]

Notes

1   This does not invalidate provisions which are normal positive discrimination for women as women, eg pregnancy, childbirth or about jobs where only women would be suitable. Act of 1970 section 6.
2   This was an amendment made in 1984 after 14 years' experience with the Act of 1970. SI 1983 No. 1794.
3   *Clay Cross (Quarry Services) Ltd v Fletcher* (1979) ICR.
4   Sex Discrimination Act 1975 section 55.
5   Sex Discrimination Act 1975 section 1.
6   *Gill v El Vino Co. Ltd* (1983) 1 AER 598.
7   Act of 1975 section 1. Lord Denning gave forceful expression to the basic principle in *Jeremiah v Ministry of Defence* (1979) ICR 13. 'Equality is the order of the day. In both directions. For both sexes.'
8   Act of 1975 section 7.
9   Act of 1975 section 44.
10   Act of 1975 Part VII section 65. Legal advice on the Legal Aid Green Form scheme may be helpful before deciding on the best step to take.
11   Act of 1975 section 17.
12   On 30 April 1985. This provides a summary showing some twenty-two offences under the Act of 1975. A major one, carrying a £2000 fine, is under

section 38 for knowingly or recklessly making a materially false or misleading statement to a publisher about the lawfulness of an advertisement.

b Race discrimination

The problem

Rowntree Mackintosh some years ago made a rule that the wearing of beards was forbidden in their food factories. Was this 'unlawful discrimination' against a Sikh who wished to work there?

The Kingston Health Authority refused to allow a Sikh trainee nurse to wear trousers in accordance with Sikh tradition and insisted on her wearing skirts and the other garments stipulated in a statutory rule as the official uniform. Was this lawful?

British Home Stores required employees to wear uniforms consisting of overall and skirt. This was detrimental to a Muslim from Pakistan who said that part of her belief was that women should not go about with legs uncovered. Was the requirement contrary to British Race Relations Law?

Definitions

A person discriminates unlawfully against another on grounds of race if he treats him less favourably than he treats another person. This is the basic principle in the Race Relations Act 1976. It is supported by another provision similar to that in the Sex Discrimination Act 1975 which we considered above. This is the applying to a person within a racial group of a condition which:

1 is to his detriment because he cannot comply with it, and
2 cannot be shown to be justifiable, apart from the racial origins of the person upon whom it is imposed, and
3 is such that the proportion of persons in that racial group is considerably smaller than the proportion not in that group who can comply.[1]

Applying the definition to the problems   In the first of the three illustrations given at the beginning of this section, the application of these definitions resulted in the rule forbidding beards being upheld on the grounds of hygiene.[2] The refusal to allow the nurse to wear trousers was also upheld on account of the statutory force of the rule and the nature of a nurse's work.[3] But the BHS rule about shop assistants was not supported in an industrial tribunal. It was held that the detriment outweighed any commercial need of the employers to protect their image. The rule was not justifiable under the Act of 1976.[4]

'Racial group'   In these cases and others, the definitions of racial group and racial grounds in the Act of 1976 have led to arguments in the Courts, especially about the nature of Sikhs and Jews. This is because 'racial' is defined as an umbrella term which comprises references to colour, race, nationality, ethnic or national origins. In the cases affecting Jews and Sikhs, the Courts had to analyse 'ethnic' in particular before agreeing that these were distinguishable racial groups.[5]

Segregation   The Act of 1976 has a special section to provide that segregating a person on racial grounds is unlawful discrimination.[6]

Someone else's colour   Another feature distinguishing race discrimination law from the sex discrimination law we looked at earlier is illustrated by the case of the white woman excluded from a public house, at the same time that the coloured men she was with were denied access. The Court of Appeal held that in those circumstances she had been discriminated against on grounds of colour.[7]

The same principle was supported when another tribunal held it to be unlawful discrimination for a white man to be dismissed for not carrying out his employer's orders to exclude young black men from the amusement centre where he worked.

Exclusions

These resemble those we found in the Sex Discrimination Act, with slight variations:

1 A drama or entertainment where authenticity called for a person of a particular racial group.
2 Being an artist's or photographer's model, on account of the need for authenticity.
3 Where the setting for the provision of food and drink requires persons of that racial group in the interests of authenticity.
4 Where the holder of the job provides persons of that particular group with personal services promoting their welfare and those services can most effectively be provided by a person of that racial group.

In considering these groups of exclusions, it is necessary to bear in mind the injunction in the Act that the racial feature must be 'a genuine occupational qualification for the job'.[8]

Common features in the Sex and Race Discrimination Acts

It may assist the reader to assimilate the pattern of the Act of 1976 by listing some of its main features which are, for all practical purposes, drawn up in similar terms to those in the Act of 1975.

1 Discrimination by employers is defined in relation to applications, appointments and dismissals.
2 Contract workers are dealt with in the same way in both Acts.
3 Discriminatory practices are defined by reference also to advertisements, giving instructions, exerting pressure, aiding unlawful acts, and liability as employer or as principal.
4 Charities are given a similar exemption in both Acts.
5 Education and training are dealt with similarly.
6 The composition and powers of the Commission for Racial Equality set up in the Act of 1976 are very similar to those in the Act of 1975 for the Equal Opportunities Commission.
7 Enforcement of the Act of 1976 follows a similar pattern to that described for the Act of 1975, with reference to County Courts, industrial tribunals, non-discrimination notices and also in connection with assistance to claimants, actual or prospective.

The reader should take note of the Code of Practice, published in May 1984 and usefully divided into the provisions respectively affecting employers, trade unions and employment agencies.

Conclusion

The reported cases about the leisure services are few and far between. It may be useful therefore to note one which reached the House of Lords, *Wheeler and others v Leicester City Council* (1985).[9]

The facts briefly were that Leicester FC were, by resolution of the Council, banned from using a recreation ground for twelve months. The background was that three members of the Club had joined a rugby tour of South Africa. The Leicester Club had expressed its own opposition to apartheid and given the three men literature on the subject. Having done that, the Club left them to make their own decisions, to go or not to go.

The Court had to decide a case brought for the removal of the ban, particularly in the light of one provision in the Act of 1976.[10] This says that local authorities should be under a duty to make arrangements with a view to securing that 'their various functions are carried out with due regard to the need:

a to eliminate unlawful racial discrimination; and
b to promote equality of opportunity, and good relations, between persons of different racial groups.'

After argument, the Court removed the ban on the ground that it was not, in the particular circumstances, a reasonable use of these statutory powers. Lord Templeman said, in one passage:

> The laws of this country were not like those laws of Nazi Germany. A private individual or private organisation could not be obliged to display zeal in the pursuit of an object sought by a public authority and could not be obliged to publish views dictated by a public authority. The club having committed no wrong, the council could not use their statutory powers in the management of their property or other statutory powers in order to punish the club. That did not mean that the council was bound to allow its property to be used by a racist organisation . . . But the attitude of the club was a perfectly proper one, caught as they were in a political controversy which was not of their making.

Notes

1 Race Relations Act 1976 section 1.
2 *Singh v Rowntree Mackintosh Ltd* (1979) ICR 554.
3 *Kingston and Richmond AHA v Kaur* (1981) ICR 631.
4 *Malik v British Home Stores* COIT 987/12.
5 The House of Lords decision in *Mandla and Mandla v Dowell Lee and Park Grove School* (1983) ICR 385 contains an authoritative judgement on the legal concept of ethnic origins. That was the case where the boy was refused a school place because he would not remove his turban and cut his hair, as required by the school rules.
6 Act of 1976 section 1.
7 *Race Relations Board v Applin* (1974) 2 AER 73.
8 Act of 1976 section 5.
9 *Wheeler and others v Leicester City Council* (1985) 3 WLR 335.
10 Act of 1976 section 71.

5 Commercial transactions and their problems

5.1 Contract

We shall consider this branch of the law by reference to:

1 Forming the contract.
2 Impediments to forming a legal contract.
3 Performing the contract.
4 The breach and its consequences.

Forming the contract

Many agreements are made daily which the parties involved do not intend to give rise to legal obligations. The mechanisms of society are oiled by amicable arrangements but 'Will you let me have an order?' . . . 'I'll write you a letter about it' and 'I think we'd better put it in writing', indicate another sort of relationship.

So the contracts we are considering here are those designed to create legal relationships and which are enforceable in the Courts. This simple statement rules out a number of incomplete arrangements, proposals which were never accepted and unlawful propositions. We will look at these situations in turn.

A legal contract comes into being when two competent parties conclude an agreement, comprising offer, acceptance and adequate consideration. The consideration is simply the return or 'quid pro quo' which is passing between the parties as a result of the agreement. It may be money, it may be money's worth as in barter or perhaps it is the cancellation of an old debt. A may supply fertiliser for B's sports field in return for the waste from B's canteen for his own piggeries.

Offer and acceptance

Offer and acceptance can cause complications for lawyers. One or two examples may be useful. Goods on display in a store with a price tag are, in law, not on offer and thereby not 'accepted' by the customer who picks them up and walks to the check-out point. It is the customer who is deemed to *offer* to buy when he presents the goods to the cashier at the point of sale;

the cashier then concludes the contract by *accepting* that offer and making the goods ready to take away. Again at an auction a bid is deemed to be an *offer* and a fall of the hammer is the *acceptance*. A bid can therefore be taken back before the hammer falls. Another instance is the case of an offer to sell made by post. This may clearly contemplate acceptance by putting a letter in the post. If that is so, then the time when the acceptance reaches the seller or, being lost in the post, the fact that the acceptance never reaches the seller becomes immaterial. The rule here is that the acceptance should be in the form contemplated by the parties. Some circumstances may therefore require a telephone call or the arrival at the seller's address of a written letter of acceptance.

The other common situation which may arise for leisure services managers is the acceptance of a tender to supply, say, food to a cafeteria over a period of time. Whether the acceptance concludes a firm, legally enforceable contract depends on the wording of the relevant documents. In some circumstances there will only be a contract each time the buyer places his weekly order for goods. In other situations, price, quality, even quantity of the goods may all be clearly settled in the tender and there will be a comprehensive contract when the tender is accepted.

We conclude this section by saying that to form a legal contract there must be parties in agreement, shown by offer, acceptance and consideration. There must also be an intention to create legal relationships. We shall be considering incapacity of the parties and unlawfulness of the object, in the next subsection. In addition, the Unfair Contract Terms Act 1977 is one of a number of special statutes which, in recent years, have altered parts of the common law on contract; we shall also be looking at that in the next section.

Impediments to forming the contract

We now look first at the capacity of the parties and the lawfulness of the objects of a contract. But another large area of law has developed about the factors which can stop the parties being legally at one, though apparently so. These are mistake, misrepresentation and duress or undue influence.

Capacity

A minor is the legal term for a person under 18 years of age. Persons entering into contracts with minors must be wary, for the law is protective of them. They are treated as responsible when entering into a contract of service, as when a young footballer signs terms with a club. Again, if they make a contract about a subject of a permanent nature like the tenancy of a flat, that is a contract which can be enforced against a minor. Moreover the contracts which a minor makes to acquire what have been called necessaries will be enforced against the minor.

It is contracts for non-necessaries which a minor can repudiate and this description is settled by the Courts in the light of the minor's social standing and social requirements. Another example of this class of contracts which the minor can legally repudiate, is when setting up in business. The law there is that the minor can enforce the contract but it cannot be enforced against him.[1]

It was in 1969 that the age of majority was lowered from 21 to 18 and this reform has greatly reduced the number of contentious minors' contracts. The modern approach is to hold the minor more and more responsible for his contracts and an Act in 1987 continued this progress.[2] It allows the Court to order the return by a minor of goods acquired even under an unenforceable contract, as mentioned above, if 'just and equitable'. This power can be used also against the traceable proceeds of what was originally acquired. So sports goods, bought but sold to raise cash, could lead to an order in respect of the known cash.

Two other situations where non-capacity might imperil a contract are, firstly, if mental illness afflicts a party and secondly, if a party is a company under the Companies Acts, and the permitted objects in its memorandum of association are breached.

Lawful objects of the contract
The Courts will not enforce contracts for unlawful objects such as keeping a brothel or incurring gaming debts. This does not of course stop people agreeing to part with money in those and other ventures: it just means that the Courts will not lend their help to either party seeking to recover money if the agreement goes sour on him. The contract, in other words, does not give rise to legal rights of enforcement for the parties to it.

Again, on account of public policy, some contracts will not be enforced because they are illegal at common law. These are ones which seek to defraud the Revenue or are prejudicial to the administration of justice, eg bribing a juror. Other instances are agreements tending to corruption in public life or in connection with committing a crime or being to the prejudice of public safety. These are wide in their terms but in practice are limited. Their wide definition allows the Courts to take account of changing attitudes in our society.

Contracts in restraint of trade
Perhaps the group of greatest interest to those engaged in the leisure services are contracts deemed to be in restraint of trade. These are of two sorts, those relating to the employee and those about a company or other trading organisation.

Employee The individual leisure services manager will inevitably acquire knowledge of trade, mark ups, discounts, availability of artistes and so on. Some of this knowledge is simple commercial expertise: some may cross the border into trade secrets. The extension of the British leisure market to Europe and the complexity of computer based data vastly increase the chance of this happening.

An employer will then insert in an employee's contract of employment a clause requiring him to keep those secrets for ever or for five years or some other restriction. For example, it might call on him not to work within 50 miles of his present employer's base. The question is whether the Courts will support such a clause if it is broken and the employer seeks to enforce it? The answer is: if it is reasonable. In assessing this, the Courts try to balance time, money and other factors. The easy example is the hall manager who agrees a high fee to an entertainer on condition that he does not perform within say 50 miles or within a month of the date in question. Whilst this could well be reasonable, another clause trying to stop a similar performance within 100 miles and six months might, in the setting of the geography of the United Kingdom, be unreasonable. Numerous cases illuminate this test in the varied situations which have arisen.

Trading agreement   This is the case of two companies agreeing perhaps not to compete in defined areas, or otherwise seeking to restrict normal trade. The Courts have grappled over the years with munitions manufacture, beer brewing, Harris tweed sales, petrol filling station restraints and many more. This common law is now however, supplemented by the Restrictive Trade Practices Acts of 1956 and 1976. These generally make unlawful collective agreements which seek to cut off supplies from those who do not comply with desired terms of trading. The Monopolies and Mergers Commission is a statutory body constituted to examine questionable contracts of this nature. Managers need to know that such an area of commercial illegality exists and to take advice about particular cases.

Mistake

There are three areas where a mistake can upset a contract; clearly a contract depends on agreement and some mistakes are so fundamental that the apparent agreement was found not to be a true one.

Mutual mistake   A mutual mistake may exist about the subject of the contract, eg the site for a new sports centre. It may be thought by both builder and employer to be sound and stable and thus needing only normal foundations. In fact it may be fissured and in need of extensive and expensive piling. Again cases have reached the Courts where two parties were in error about the true artist of a painting being bought and sold. Such a contract is not inherently bad or void: it is said to be voidable. This means that the parties can either set it aside and start again or rectify it.

Unilateral mistake   Where, on the other hand, one party is mistaken and the other party is aware of this but does not enlighten him, this is called 'unilateral mistake'. The aggrieved party may be deceived by false letter heads, or even about the true name of the party he is dealing with. The law is that he can have the contract set aside in the Courts if he shows that he took reasonable means to establish the truth of the item about which he was mistaken, that it was an important item in relation to the contract and, thirdly, that the other party knew of his error.

Mistaken document   Documents are sometimes signed under a mistake about their effect. The Courts are reluctant to tear up such a document. A man is expected to know what he is signing, they say, and so they give no comfort for mere carelessness. But to ask a man to sign, saying that he is witnessing a Will, when the document is a mortgage, is clearly a fraud and the contract can be rescinded. The trouble is that the cases which reach the

Courts are usually more finely balanced between mistake and carelessness. Only when the Courts are satisfied that the person who signed failed to understand the *nature of the document* he was signing because of mental incapacity, illness or some other special disability, will the Courts be inclined to relieve him of the consequences of this type of mistake.

Misrepresentation

When, before the contract is made, a party makes a statement of fact which is not true and is crucial to the contract, that can be a misrepresentation in law. An opinion, also, can be a misrepresentation, if it purports to be based on facts which the maker knows are not true. It is essential, in order for an aggrieved party to show that he was induced by a misrepresentation to enter into a contract, to satisfy the Court that he *relied* upon the misrepresentation. Suppose a developer of a new swimming pool is given a catchment area appraisal by the site owner to show the attractions of the locality, but the appraisal is specious and omits relevant facts. However, the developer obtains his own survey and relies upon that when deciding to buy the site and develop; clearly the defective report did not *induce* the developer to sign and pay. Thus he could not seek relief under this part of the law of contract.

The relevant principles are these:

1 A misrepresentation made fraudulently can be relied upon by the aggrieved party in order to sue for rescission of the contract and compensation in the form of damages.

2 The Misrepresentation Act 1967 allows the same remedy for innocent misrepresentation. This misrepresentation can be a statement, it can be conduct and occasionally it can be silence.

3 However the plaintiff must be able to show that he was induced by the misrepresentation to enter into the contract. If he delays unduly, or even treats the contract as valid, so that it could be said that he had *affirmed* it, then he cannot get rescission in the Courts. He is also refused rescission if it is impossible to restore the pre contract situation, eg if a building has been demolished to prepare the building site. The fourth and last case where rescission is not given, is where third parties in good faith and for value have entered into the situation. Perhaps they have bought the secondhand multi-gym or other valuable equipment and they would be adversely affected by rescission. In that case also, recission is not available; the aggrieved must sue for damages alone. We emphasise that rescission as a remedy is discretionary.

Undue influence

The last situation to consider, where apparent agreement is found to be specious, is where one of the parties acted under undue influence in entering into the contract. This could be physical, eg by being drugged or captured and held to ransom, or it might be emotional, eg by falsely creating fears of the consequences if he did not sign. The Courts look for two elements before setting aside a contract on this ground. The first is that the contract signed is to the disadvantage of the plaintiff. The second is that the influence, however exerted, resulted in a person's will being dominated or overcome by the other so that it did not freely lead him into the contract. The cases in the reports mostly involve commerce, such as money from banks or building societies or the terms for shipping adventures. However a recent case from the entertainment field is _Sullivan v Management Agency & Music Ltd_ (1984).[3] Here a composer and performer of popular music signed a series of agreements for the promotion of his music by publishing and by records. He became very successful. However he had taken no independent advice before following the guidance of his agent to enter into these agreements, in which his interests were not as well served as might otherwise have occurred. So he sought and obtained a declaration in the Courts that the agreements were void. The Court of Appeal said that the agent was in a fiduciary position to Sullivan; the latter was trusting the agent to the extent that his free will and independent judgement were overborne in the transactions which he was persuaded to engage in.

Performing the contract

When a contract to build a new swimming pool is under way, an architect for the buyer will check the progress of the work against the contract. In doing so, he will liaise with the builder's own architect. Variations of all sorts will occur as the contract proceeds and will be recorded in notices of variation, be they for the style of pendant lamps or the colour of facing bricks or many other items. A building inspector will also, independently, be checking compliance of the work with building regulations.

But the law contributes one or two important elements to this question.

Assignment

A party can assign his interest in a contract. He may well be required by the contract to notify the other party: it is always wise to do so. Then the assignee steps into the shoes of the assignor.

This right, though appropriate for the above swimming pool, does not exist when the contract is of a personal nature. If a football development coach is appointed by a local authority, it will doubtless be on account of his personal qualities. It is against reason and is also against the law for such a person to be able, without consent, to assign and say 'Gilbert will finish off this contract for me'.

Privity of contract

This is an ancient legal rule, that only parties to a contract can sue about its provisions. Take as an example _Tweddle v Atkinson_ (1861).[4] The fathers of a bride and bridegroom agreed that each would make payments to the happy couple. One did but one didn't. In Court it was held that the groom could not sue, since he was not one of the parties to the contract.

But the doctrine is not universal. For instance, the Road Traffic Act 1972 (section 149) covers the situation where a stranger to a contract between a motorist and his insurance company is permitted to sue that insurance company, in certain circumstances. Another allied act is the Third Parties (Rights Against Insurers) Act 1930 which was specially enacted to let a party outside the contract between the motorist and his insurance company, viz an injured pedestrian, sue the insurance company if the individual motorist, who was really liable, became bankrupt or, if it was a company car, the company had gone into liquidation.

These illustrations show how the legislature was used to make clear certain rights and obligations which cut across the initial common law rules.

There are other exceptions about land, bills of exchange and shipping – all somewhat remote from leisure service managers.

Substantial performance

Some contracts are by their nature fulfilled quickly; you buy a piano and it is delivered. Hopefully, that is that. But building and other contracts take time. It is for these that the law has developed the concept of substantial performance. This is the point when the purpose of the building is substantially achieved, so that the last major payment can be safely made to the builder and possession taken by the purchaser. There will still be some finishing off to be done and some tidying up but the main purpose of the contract has been fulfilled. The doctrine came into existence to mitigate a previous harsh rule that denied the builder his payment or the supplier his contractual money until every little item was complete.

Frustration

This is more complex; it deals with the legal treatment of the situation when the contract cannot be performed due to some unexpected event. It rained; or the ship sank; or the singer got laryngitis. Again the law has developed in recent years to ameliorate rules which used to be somewhat harsh.

The Law Reform (Frustrated Contracts) Act 1943 allows monies paid before the frustrating event to be recovered. This is subject to a deduction of agreed expenses incurred by the other party. In the case of work performed before that event, a quantum meruit payment is then allowed, ie a reasonable recompense for the time, labour and materials expended up to that time, called 'the time of discharge' in the above Act of 1943.

This Act has set the ground rules for resolving what can be difficult problems for all involved. There are perhaps two final points to emphasise. Firstly, it is not simply difficulties in performance that justify a claim that the contract has been frustrated. If the circus comes to town and performs, it is doubtless distressing that the elephants were ill and hors de combat but, unless the Court holds otherwise, there is still a circus and a performance is possible. However, when a solo pianist takes to his bed the concert may just have to be cancelled and this Act is used to sort out the consequences. Secondly, the modern approach of the Courts to the frustration situation is to devise a just solution to the problem, taking account of what both parties have committed and suffered and the nature of the frustrating event.

Breach and its consequences

Remedies

There are three legal remedies for a breach of contract:

1 *Damages* is the normal one. It is comprised of that sum which represents the financial consequences to the plaintiff which are deemed to arise naturally from the breach. This is subject to the plaintiff taking reasonable steps to 'mitigate his loss'. Also, the probable consequences of a breach have to be known at the time of making the contract. This element depends on communication, as discussed below.

2 *Quantum meruit*, the technical term still used to describe that sum of money which is as much as he deserves. It is to compensate for the value of work and other items expended before the breach and including the benefit, if appropriate to the subject matter, conferred on the property. It is an alternative to damages depending on the nature of the contract.

3 *Specific performance* is appropriate to some breaches but not others. It is discretionary whilst damages are a right. It is used where damages are not thought by the Court to be, on their own, an adequate remedy for the injury caused by the breach. It is not used if the performance of the contract had an essentially personal character to it and that is, in the circumstances, no longer available. Nor is it used if it would be too complex to carry out.

Damages

With regards to damages, it does not avail a party to say, for the first time, after the breach 'What a shame. I was depending on that equipment to promote my new company in Patagonia. I have lost £1m in consequence of the breach'. In other words, the expected consequences, touched on in 1 above, in order to be taken into account by a Court assessing damages, have to be known to both parties. Items disallowed from inclusion in the damages calculation like the Patagonian adventure, are said, technically, to be too remote.

Thus the rules about damages may be summarised as follows:

1 The purpose of damages is to put the injured party, so far as money can do so, in the same position as if the contract has been performed.

2 The injured party has to 'mitigate his loss'. This means taking such reasonable steps as he can to control escalation of the expected damages. If the goods lorry broke down or the ship's engine failed, this could mean chartering another lorry or ship to try to achieve delivery sooner rather than later.

3 The contract may possibly include a genuine pre-estimate of damage, eg 'If the 50 houses being built are not completed and handed over by 31 May, then the builder will pay XYZ Ltd a sum calculated at the rate of £40 per house per week in respect of houses not handed over, such sum representing the estimated loss of rent suffered by XYZ Ltd from the said delay', ie if the possible breach occurred. The Courts will enforce such a contracted figure. What they will *not* enforce is a figure, ostensibly of the same nature, but in reality a *penalty* for delay or other breach. The Court would look at the whole circumstances before deciding if the sum was merely a non-enforceable penalty or a genuine pre-estimate of damage.

Two cases from the theatre and cinema worlds may help in drawing the curtain on what is admittedly a complicated branch of contract law. In 1829 the famous actor Kemble agreed to appear at a theatre for four seasons. He was to be paid £3 6s 8d per day. The contract said that if either party defaulted £1000 was payable to the other. Following a breach, the case came into Court and it was held that the £1000 was a penalty: such a large sum in relation to the daily small sums must have that character (*Kemble v Farren* (1829)).[5]

On the other hand, a film actress, Bette Davis, agreed to perform exclusively for Warner Bros. On breaking her contract but able to carry on working, the Court granted an injunction to compel her to honour her contract. The equitable remedy of specific performance seemed suitable in that situation (*Warner Bros. Inc v Nelson* (1937)).[6]

Notes

1 Voidable at the instance of the minor, is the legal technical language.
2 Minors' Contracts Act 1987 section 3. A century old act, of which the title indicates the approach of the law, was the Infants Relief Act 1874. This was repealed by this Act of 1987.
3 *Sullivan v Management Agency & Music Ltd* (1984) Law Soc. Gazette 3 December 1984 p 2693.
4 *Tweddle v Atkinson* (1861) 1861–73 AER 369.
5 *Kemble v Farren* (1829) 1824–34 AER 641.
6 *Warner Bros. Inc v Nelson* (1937) 1 KB 209.

5.2 Unfair Contract Terms Act 1977

This Act is best considered against the backcloth of the general law of contract which has been considered above, rather than woven into it.

Purpose

As the title tells us, it is intended to impose limits on the extent to which civil liability for breach of contract or negligence can be avoided by terms in a contract. It is a complex Act, though not very long. We select the provisions which bear on the leisure services and their management.

1 The Act deals with contractual duties of a business nature.
2 The duties in question are:
   a To exercise reasonable care in the execution of a contract.
   b The Common Law duty of reasonable care.
   c The Common duty of care under the Occupiers Liability Act 1957. (The later Occupiers Liability Act of 1984 makes specific reference to visitors for recreational or educational purposes, when those activities form part of the business of the occupier. The 1984 Act then precludes the occupier from limiting his occupier's liability for the dangerous state of the premises.)
3 The two main provisions are in section 2 of the Act of 1977:

Death and personal injury
First, if death or personal injury has resulted from the negligence of the defendant, that defendant cannot rely on a contract term or notice to exclude or restrict his legal liability. So if, during a thunderstorm, a dangerous elm tree fell and killed a visitor enjoying a round of golf on a municipal course, the manager could not derive legal protection from a clause on the back of the receipt ticket which purported to exclude liability for injury due to Act of God. His liability would fall to be decided on the other general principles of negligence, ie should he have reasonably foreseen this danger?

Damage and the reasonable test
Secondly, where neither death nor personal injury resulted but other damage was caused by, say, the elm falling on a visitor's car, the Act of 1977 says that the liability of the defendant is to depend upon the test of reasonableness. This is an interesting provision, dealt with in section 11 and amplified in schedule II. Section 11 says the term shall have been a fair and reasonable one to be included (ie in the contract) 'having regard to the circumstances which were or ought reasonably to have been known to or in the contemplation of the parties, when the contract was made'.

Schedule II then provides that the reasonableness test is to take account of the relative bargaining positions of the parties, how far one of the parties had been induced to enter into the contract, how far a customer knew or ought to have known of the term if exclusion depended on a condition, how far the condition was practicable and whether goods were specifically adapted to the customer in question.

A recent case concerned a person who gave in a film for developing. It was a special film with shots of a silver wedding and the developer lost it. He tried, in Court, to rely on an exemption clause and refund only the cost of the film. He had printed on the trade envelope, 'We will undertake further liability at a supplementary charge. Details on request'. The Court did not accept that this passed the reasonableness test, set out above, in the Act of 1977. It should at the very least have plainly set out the alternatives so that the customer could take a reasoned decision, ie on whether to pay the supplementary charge for the extra cover. So the customer got £50 damages, and, equally important, his costs (*Warren v Truprint Ltd* (1986)).[1]

4 The Act also prohibits those specious guarantees which take away more than they give. So a 'guarantee' cannot take away liability for defective goods supplied to a customer or responsibility for negligence in manufacture or distribution of the goods (section 5).

5 *Exclusions*

It has to be emphasised that the Act does not affect clauses in contracts about insurance, land, patents or copyrights, and similar items, nor about company formation and disbanding.

6 *'As a consumer'*

Lastly, a leisure service manager may come across exception clauses in a contract to supply him with goods. These clauses also have to pass the reasonableness test if the party paying for the goods is not in the position of a consumer as the 1977 Act defines it. If he is in that position, then such exclusions are prohibited absolutely (section 7).

This expression 'as a consumer' is related to the wish of Parliament to give protection to a person in a consumer role against one selling in a business role. An example of this concept of 'consumer' was given in *Peters v Cook* (1981). It was held that a partnership of accountants which bought a car was, in that transaction, a 'consumer', since car buying was not the business they were in.

In conclusion, it may be helpful to quote a sentence from Lord Diplock, in a famous case which indicates the strong support for this Act. He pithily described the party with superior bargaining power as one who is able to say: 'If you want these goods or services at all, these are the only terms on which they are available. Take it or leave it' (*A. Schroeder Music Publishing Co. Ltd v Macaulay* (1974)).[2] It is this Act, in its sophisticated way, which makes great inroads in that impermissible stance.

Notes

1   *Warren v Truprint Ltd* (1986) BTLC 344.
2   *A. Schroeder Music Publishing Co. Ltd v Macaulay* (1974) 3 AER 616.

5.3 Consumer protection

This expression has become as much of an umbrella term as leisure services itself. It is the result on the one hand of the complexity of our consumer society and, on the other, of the organisation of consumers as a group in our society. The resulting law seeks to balance the welfare of consumers against the need to encourage producers.

It is found in the Statute Book in a sequence of Acts about fair trading, fair marketing of goods and services, the protection of consumers against unsafe goods and also against unfair terms of credit in sales by hire purchase. In 1987 the major Consumer Protection Act was in part a response to a European Community (EC) Directive on product liability and in part a consolidation of proliferating legislation. In short the topic is very much alive and we look at it in the convenient divisions of product liability and consumer safety; fair trading; trade descriptions; supply of goods and services; and consumer credit.

Product liability

The Consumer Protection Act 1987 Part I embodies the UK Law designed to implement the requirements of an EC Directive on product liability. Article I provides, with beguiling simplicity 'The producer shall be liable for damage caused by a defect in his product'.

We say 'beguiling' for the Article is only understood when the complex definitions of the producer, damage, defect and producer are examined. The Act could relate, among a myriad other items, to the football, diving board or baseball bat meant for private use. We proceed accordingly to summarise the main points of interest in the field of public leisure services.

Damage
The only 'damage' covered by the Act of 1987 is death, personal injury (which includes disease and impairment of a person's physical or mental condition, section 45) and also loss or damage to property exceeding £275. The property in question has to be intended by the person suffering the damage to be for his own use, occupation or consumption.

Persons liable
The persons liable are the producer of the article in question, the ostensible producer (sometimes called 'the marker' since he has his own name on the product, though it was produced by someone else), and thirdly, the person who imported it into the EC to supply it in course of business.

Defect
The Act is primarily about defects which relate to safety; 'if the safety of the product is not such as persons generally are entitled to expect' (section 3) is the critical description. The defect must be shown to be in the product; the Court cannot rely on inference for this crucial element.

Defences
There are six statutory defences, so many indeed that it has been said that they undermine the Act.

1 That the defect is due to the supplier complying with an EC requirement.
2 That the supplier did not supply the product to 'another' ie another consumer. In other words, it was an isolated transaction.
3 That though there was a supply to 'another' the product was not acquired by that other in the course of business.
4 That the defect did not exist in the product at the time when it was supplied.
5 That the state of knowledge when the product was supplied was such that the producer would not be expected to have discovered the defect if then present. (The supplier has to prove this.)
6 That the product for which the supplier is responsible was a part only of the larger product as supplied to the claimant. And that his part in the whole was due to the design requirements of the subsequent producer.

It should be noted that liability under the Act cannot be limited or excluded by notice or contract term or otherwise.

Consumer safety

Now contained in Part II of the Consumer Protection Act 1987, this aspect of consumer protection was formerly in two earlier Acts.[1]

General safety principles
Section 10 of the main Act of 1987 now sets out a general safety requirement, breach of which is an offence. This consists in the 'supplying, possessing for supply and agreeing to supply, consumer goods which fail to comply with the general requirement'. The Act then describes aspects of goods which may indicate this failure:

1 The manner of their marketing, 'the get-up of the goods', to quote the jargon in the Act.
2 The contents of relevant standards of safety for those goods.
3 The existence of means to make those goods safer.

Goods shall not be regarded as failing to comply with the general safety requirement simply because more has not been done by the supplier than is required in relation to their safety by various types of law.

Defences
Finally, section 10 provides three defences against a prosecution:

1 That the supplier reasonably believed that the goods would not be used or consumed in the UK.
2 That he was handling the goods in his retail business and had no reason to suspect that they fell below the safety standard.
3 That the goods were not being supplied as new goods and the person supplied was expected to acquire an interest in them.

Further, a general defence of due diligence is available when prosecuted. This means that he took all reasonable steps and exercised all due diligence to avoid committing an offence. Sanctions for one of these offences are fines and imprisonment.

The Act then sets this general safety principle in the framework of powers for the Secretary of State to make safety regulations and issue prohibition notices about designated goods. Other legal weapons available are notices to warn – issued when dangerous goods are already in a chain of distribution and obliging the head of the chain to warn all in the chain about the danger. The Weights and Measures authority are empowered to serve suspension notices (section 14) to stop the distribution of named goods.

Appeals against these executive steps may be taken to Magistrates Courts. Those Courts can themselves order the forfeiture of goods, where a contravention of a relevant safety provision is proved.

Fair trading

It was the Fair Trading Act of 1973 which set up the Director General of Fair Trading and a Consumer Protection Advisory Committee. Though the Committee recently lapsed the Director General is an active part of the consumer protection scene. He maintains surveillance over suspect commercial activities and collects information about practices which may adversely affect the rights of consumers. He reports regularly to the Secretary of State and submits a formal annual report, which is published.[2] He is given directions on priorities in these activities and is able to take action against those responsible for actions detrimental to the interests of consumers and regarded as unfair to them.

In addition to this activity on what may be called the strategic front, the Director General engages in detailed enforcement of fair trading with individual traders. He may prosecute them for 'adverse practices'; this means persisting 'in a course of conduct which is detrimental to consumers' and is unfair to them. Cases go before the Restrictive Practices Court, with a right of appeal to the Court of Appeal.

Finally, the Office of Fair Trading promulgates Codes of Practice, which set out best practices in specified areas of commerce. Recent ones concerned travel agents and holiday caravans.[3]

Trade descriptions

The current law on this aspect of our subject is in the Trade Description Act 1968 and Part III of the Consumer Protection Act 1987. There are three main offences created in these Acts:

1 Applying a false trade description to goods, in the course of a trade or business (Act of 1968 section 1).

2 Supplying or offering to supply goods to which a false trade description has been applied, again, in the course of a trade or business (Act of 1968 section 1).

3 Giving to consumers a misleading price indication in the course of a business. This offence is set out in comprehensive terms, so that it covers the situation where a price indication initially correctly given, has become misleading

with the passage of time (Act of 1987 section 20). Another section deals in detail with the meaning of 'misleading' for purposes of this offence.

Primarily about 'goods', the Act does apply for example to car park and caravan parking spaces, being examples of services and facilities. It does not, however, extend to contracts of employment and has only a limited application to real property.

Defences

The defences in the Act of 1968 to the first two offences listed above are these:

1 It was an accident.
2 It was a mistake.
3 It was due to another person.
4 It was done in reliance on information supplied.
5 It was due to some cause outside his control.

In addition, the defendant must show that, so far as he was concerned, he did all he could to avoid the commission of the offence in question (Trade Description Act 1968 section 24).

Finally, it may be expected that the Secretary of State will not only promulgate a Code of Practice about best practice in the field of price indications but also make regulations about ways in which price indications may be given and the law enforced.

Supply of goods and services

Some contracts needed in the field of leisure services, like a new set of tennis courts or a trim trail, have the characteristic that both a supply of goods and the provision of building services are involved. Because legislation was effective about sales of goods but weak about these sort of dual contracts, Parliament enacted the Goods and Services Act 1982, the main features of which we now summarise.

Implied conditions

Such contracts are deemed to contain four conditions, viz that the supplier has a sound title to the goods, that those goods conform with any contracted description, that they comply with the standard of *merchantable quality* (as explained in the section below about the Sale of Goods Act, where the expression originates), and fourthly, in so far as the goods were illustrated at tendering stage by a sample, that the bulk is in accordance with the sample and two statutory terms about samples are fulfilled.[4]

Furthermore, these four conditions are also imported by the Act of 1982 into contracts for the hiring of goods (sections 7–10).

Contracts for services

Examples of these are servicing motor vehicles or erecting scaffolding. What this Act does is to import into these contracts three terms, viz

1 The service will be carried out with reasonable care and skill;

2 It will be done in a reasonable time;
3 A reasonable charge will be paid for the service, 'reasonable' in each instance being interpreted in relation to the circumstances.

Excluded contracts (part I)
These are hire purchase agreements, contracts only for the sale of goods, trading stamp transfer agreements and contracts with no consideration but enforceable because sealed.

Let the buyer beware
Though there is now the condition about merchantable quality, this does not coddle the buyer in a situation where he has had a chance to form his own judgement and decided to act on it. In particular, where he actually inspected, he must stand the risk of a defect that the inspection would have revealed to him if he had displayed normal prudence. Likewise, when the vendor has drawn attention to a defect, the purchaser is deemed to take that into account when settling the terms of the contract.

Title
The vendor may know of a third party's interest in the goods part of the contract and thus wish to qualify his obligation about having a first class title. Perhaps, in a fanciful illustration, he had given a friend a promise of the use of several boats being furnished in a new marina, if and when the friend became qualified to take part in a special race, and that this arrangement would only last for 12 months. Then the Act says that the vendor can give a warranty, rather than a condition, about this but he must disclose in full the charge or third party interest. We are into another legal balancing act.

Excluded contracts (part II)
Apprenticeships, contracts of service and services specified in orders are excluded from services under this Act.[5]

Consumer credit

The Consumer Credit Act 1974 is the current legal point of reference on this complex topic. With twelve parts and nearly 200 sections, it has been brought into force slowly and replaces earlier laws about hire purchase, money lenders and pawnbrokers. For those engaged in the public leisure services, it should suffice to be aware of the main provisions in this Act:

1 The Director General of Fair Trading is given a major role to administer the licensing of consumer credit and consumer hire businesses.
2 Formalities are prescribed to govern regulated credit and regulated hire agreements. These permit withdrawal and cancellation in certain circumstances.
3 The suppliers of goods are brought under legal control in relation to misrepresentation in breach of their contracts.
4 There are strict controls on the securities that can be used in relation to credit for consumers.

5 The County Courts have wide powers about regulated agreements. These include making 'time orders' under which a debtor is given time to pay or otherwise remedy a default. The Courts can also re-open extortionate credit agreements.

Notes

1 The Consumer Safety Act 1978 and the Consumer Safety (Amendment) Act 1986. This was used as a staging post by the draftsmen to gather the new items which, with the Act of 1978, were to be consolidated in Part II of the Act of 1987.
2 The Annual report for 1986 lists 22 people who gave formal section 34 assurances and one who gave such an assurance to the Court. 555 assurances are said to have been obtained since the law allowed that step.
3 The next two are said, in the 1986 report, to relate to timber treatment and damp proof courses.
4 The other two conditions are that inspection of the sample will reveal any defect of a nature such as to render the goods unmerchantable and, secondly, that the buyer will have an opportunity to compare bulk with sample.
5 Two early orders specified the services of an advocate and those of a director of a building society – both somewhat removed from leisure services.

5.4 Commercial agency

There are a number of situations where the word 'agent' is loosely used. Here we limit our consideration to the legal situation, where an agent has authority to enter into legal relations between two other persons. One is his principal and the other is some third party. So if the 'agent' is in a situation where he is acting on his own behalf, he is not in a true legal agency situation. Clearly the existence of an agreement between the principal and the agent is essential and we shall consider how far the absence of an express or written agreement may be supplemented by an implied agreement. In the entertainment world, managers may deal frequently with artistes, group and orchestra agents, and will occasionally, perhaps reluctantly, have to appoint an agent themselves. We try to point out the danger points in these situations.

The four other aspects of a commercial agency which we shall mention are:

1 The situation of an agent acting for a principal who himself has not due legal capacity, eg he is under age for legal contracts.
2 The need for ratification of an agent's acts.
3 The effect on a third person of fraud by an agent.
4 The termination of an agency.

Formation of an agency

The terms of the agency may be straightforward when in writing or, possibly, created by power of attorney.[1] This is the name of the document, now regulated by statute, which appoints the agent to manage the affairs of the principal either generally or for the purposes of a named transaction. It is often used if a principal is to be absent abroad or otherwise from his place of business for some time. Such a document should be formally signed and witnessed, as required by the statute. In the local authority situation, a person would act as agent in accordance with their standing orders.

Sometimes and in a very limited number of cases, an agency is deemed to exist 'of necessity'. For instance in a shipwreck, the captain could act as agent for the owners, though normally he would simply be one of their employees. This would only happen if the principal could not be contacted, and the agent was considered to have taken the only prudent course, eg in agreeing to be salvaged or perhaps lightening the cargo. The third condition is that the agent of necessity acted bona fide in the interests of the parties concerned.

The law implies authority in an agent to perform acts necessary and incidental to his main task.

Principal without legal capacity

Since the agent stands in the place of his principal, normally if the principal has no legal capacity, then the mere fact of being his agent cannot make good that defect. Again statute may require a person to discharge a duty himself, so that he has no power to delegate that duty to an agent. The agent, even if so described, would be no agent in law. Agents of persons intoxicated or suffering mental illness may need to show that their authority was conferred during a lucid interval of their principal.

Need for ratification of an agent's acts

The third party who enters into a contract, eg for ice cream kiosk provision on the sea front during the season, may be told that the agent's contract has to be ratified. That is a clear situation. If however such an agent had no authority and his principal did not know of the terms discussed, what then? The law is that an agent's contract may be ratified retrospectively by the principal, if done in a reasonable time.

Of course, if the act of the agent is unlawful, no amount of ratification can make it lawful. In this connection, unlawful contracts could include a case of forgery, or a gaming contract or one *ultra vires* a company with limited powers.

Effect on third party of agent's fraud

Where the third party discovers fraud or misrepresentation by the agent, eg by an estate agent concerning the number and amount of bids for property, he has the right of rescinding the agreement or accepting it and suing for damages. These alternatives were considered in the earlier section on contract and are governed largely by the Misrepresentation Act 1967.

Another aspect of this area of agency is the reliance that third parties can place on communications with an agent. The knowledge of the agent is normally deemed to be the knowledge of the principal and this doctrine would extend to, say, notices about time limits given to the agent. This would vary however if the agent had only limited authority.

Termination of an agency

An agency may end by act of the parties. It could also end by expiry of a stated period of time or perhaps by complete performance of the transaction for which the agent was appointed.

But where an auctioneer signed a memorandum a week after an auction had ended, his authority as agent for the owner of goods in the auction was held to have ended at the time of the auction. Again, if the effective operation of the agency depends on communications between principal and agent, and the principal becomes ill and hors de combat, the agency is deemed to be at an end.

Again, the bankruptcy of a principal will normally end an agency.

Note

1 Powers of Attorney Act 1971.

5.5 Insurance

Insurance law became part of the Law Merchant 300 years ago and with the rest of that law underwent codifying and reform under Lord Mansfield, the famous Lord Chief Justice at the end of the eighteenth century. It now stands on its own as a branch of our law and can best be considered here by looking a little more closely first at general principles, then at property insurance and lastly at liability insurance. To select in this way those aspects of greatest interest to those in the leisure services does mean forgoing an examination of marine, aviation and motor insurance, insurance against personal accidents, the statutory and other law about life insurance, pecuniary and war risks insurance and the regulation of insurance brokers. It should suffice to know that those areas of insurance law can be studied if desired.

General principles

Insurance has been defined as a contract by which one party (the insurer) undertakes to indemify another party (the insured) against loss, in consideration of the payment of a premium. In other words, a sum of money is to be paid by the insurer to the insured on the happening of an uncertain event. This is so, whether that event is a fire, or a disaster at sea, or whether the uncertainty consists of the length of a person's life, to take three simple examples.

There must next be an insurable interest in the assured.[1] This may be thought obvious but it is not always so. It clearly precludes taking out life insurance on a third person so that the insured premium payer has a financial incentive to shorten the life of the third person.[2]

The character of an insurance policy is an indemnity for the insured against some loss. The loss is the loss sustained: that is the essence of an indemnity. In practice the loss for example of a sports centre by fire is quantified into a certain sum when the policy is made. That still preserves the indemnity principle: it means only that the parties have avoided a delay factor in valuation which could arise if the building was destroyed.

Lastly, good faith is regarded as an integral principle of insurance law. Anything that might possibly be relevant must be disclosed to the insurer. Not to do so can make a policy void. So, for example, non-disclosure of the special piled foundations (to overcome fissures) of the swimming pool or the peril involved in its spun fibre roof might jeopardise the cover afforded by the policy against collapse or fire of that building. Again a previous refusal of insurance is regarded as a relevant matter to disclose to an insurer in the two areas of law which we are considering.

Property insurance

This can be conveniently looked at in relation to fire insurance; burglary, theft and fraud insurance; and miscellaneous peril.

Fire insurance
This is a mainstay of property management. The insurer must expect the pol-

icy to exclude certain perils, such as war, civil commotion and explosion. He must allow for the fact that if he had to claim under the policy, he would have to show ignition, and not just smoke or smouldering, and secondly, he would have to show that all the loss was as a result of the fire. For instance, falling upper walls might damage perhaps the ground floor more than the initial fire did. Nevertheless as consequential loss from the fire, the ground floor damage would be treated as a loss under the policy.

In one strange case,[3] a lady, nervous about her jewellery, wrapped it in paper and hid it under the coal and wood which was ready for lighting the fire in her grate. On her return, forgetfully, she lit the fire, damaged the jewellery but successfully claimed £460 from the insurance company. It did not matter, said the Court, if the fire went to the property or the property went to the fire: the policy covered property which was not intended to be ignited.[4]

The amount recoverable under the policy is the sum insured. This applies even though the loss is greater than that sum. It also involves the claimant in satisfying the insurance company that he has lost at least the amount insured. Unless the policy says so, the company cannot insist on another way of fulfilling their duty under the policy, eg by reinstating the property.

On the other hand, there is a statute, the Fire Prevention (Metropolis) Act 1774, found in practice to refer to the whole of England and Wales, which allows a claimant for money under a fire policy to choose as an alternative to require the company to reinstate his premises. If he does this, the company cannot be called on to spend more than the sum insured.

Burglary, theft and fraud insurance

These are items found in the criminal law and so the meanings given to them in that branch of the law will be used in interpreting an insurance policy about these risks. The normal exceptions will again be war and also items that would come in another policy, such as breakage of glass or fire. The exceptions may also cover crimes committed with the aid of specified persons, such as members of the insured's household, or perhaps in the case of leisure service managers, their staff. With a burglary policy, the insured must expect to be called on to take reasonable precautions to make his property safe.

Miscellaneous property insurance

In some locations, managers may wish to effect special property insurance. This could be against the risk of flooding or subsidence or boiler explosion. The terms would then be specially negotiated but might prove to be commercially sound investments for the premiums involved. Again, some swimming pools have a whole side wall made of plate glass and a special policy should make sense.

In the whole field, it has to be noted that many local authorities carry their own insurance. They calculate that the cost of annual premiums is more than the average cost of normal claims and so the risk of not insuring externally can be justified. Auditors would be expected to scrutinise such a decision and prompt a review if thought unrealistic.

Liability insurance

General

Leisure service managers are among those who have to organise outdoor events which can be financially disastrous if cancelled due to the weather. An insurance policy can be a useful safety net in such a situation.

There are cases in the reports about coronation processions affected by the weather and also about a notable cancellation of the Spithead Review of the Fleet.[5] One case specifically about the insurance policy in a leisure service setting was *Captain Boynton's World Water Show Syndicate v Employers Liability Assurance Corporation Ltd.*[6] A manager of a lake at Earl's Court laid out a water slide down which boats came and then at the bottom of the slide, they shot across the lake. One hazard of this operation was that they could bump into water bicycles already on the lake; in this case that is what happened, causing a passenger to break a leg. The claim on the insurance company was contested and the Court had to decide if, though the channel or chute boat as it was called, was not damaged, there had been an accident to the chute boat for that was what the policy covered. It was clear that there had been an accident affecting the water bicycle. In due course, the Court held that there had been such an accident and the company must pay. The case only reached that stage because the wording of the policy had some element of ambiguity; with a negotiated policy in particular, it behoves the insured party to be absolutely sure that he gets all the cover he needs. The cover might be full or it might be partial, it might indeed be limited to a certain number of claims in a stated period.

Such a policy should also cover costs incurred by the insured. A policy will normally allow the company if they so wish to handle any legal claim against a third party themselves, instead of leaving that matter to the insured person. But the company may not always do this.

Special

Public liability insurance is a specialised term and refers to the liability in law to members of the public.[7] These might be visitors to a public entertainment or a sporting occasion. Apart from physical injuries, such a policy might be drawn to cover also risks arising from food or drink poisoning.

Notes

1 ie The person who is the subject of the insurance policy as in a life policy.
2 The Life Assurance Act 1774.
3 *Harris v Poland* (1941) AER 204.
4 In a marine insurance policy at any rate the fire deliberately started by a stranger to the policy, has been held within the fire risk clause. *Slattery v Mance* (1962) 1 QB 676 followed in 1988 (the Alexion Hope) *The Times* 5 January 1988.
5 *Herne Bay Steam Boat Co. v Hutton* (1903) 2 KB 283; *Elliot v Critchley* (1906).
6 (1895) 11 TLR 384.
7 The claims arising from the Bradford football stadium fire would be of this nature.

5.6 Sale of goods

In a case in 1986 a farmer sued the suppliers of a herbicide in order to recover the wasted costs and anticipated profit after he had sprayed 8000 acres of winter wheat in accordance with misleading instructions. He won. At the heart of an interesting case was the finding, by the Court of Appeal, that the Sale of Goods Act 1979 section 14 applied to the transaction. When 'goods' were sold to the farmer, said the Court, the packaging and instructions for use were all parts of the 'goods'. The plaintiff had read these as an experienced and reasonable farmer and had then used the spray in June after an extremely wet spring. It did not achieve the desired result. The section of the Act of 1979 imported an implied warranty into the transaction, viz that the goods were 'reasonably fit for the purpose' for which they were sold. These were not, due to those defective instructions. The Court said that the manufacturers knew that due to the wet ground the spray could not be used effectively at all at that time.[1]

Act of 1979

The Sale of Goods Act 1893 is one of a small number of statutes which stand apart as a compact, lucid and effective codification of an important branch of our law. It is true that it was given 'a dust and a polish' when it became the present Act of 1979 but amendments of the Act of 1893 were few. The Act of 1979 accordingly deals with the total legal implications of the sale of goods.

This means the formation of the contract, the conditions and warranties implied in it, the circumstances when the buyer and seller have statutory rights against each other for things that have gone wrong, the point at which the ownership passes from one to the other, the rule about purchases by sample and finally, the rights to ask for a contract to be rescinded or to sue for damages.

The pre-eminent nature of this Act of 1979 is worth emphasis. It can be seen from Wormell's case and others how very much alive it is in litigation today. Another reason for making this point is that a cluster of special statutes in recent years has reformed the law about certain aspects of commercial transactions, so that a newcomer might be forgiven for regarding them as of equal importance.[2]

Fit for the consumer
Before describing the essential elements in the Act of 1979, reference to another recent case may be illuminating for leisure service managers. The manufacturers of a chemical sold it to a firm in business in Kuwait. It was left in containers in the sun and in due course because of the heat the contents were completely useless; the plastic containers disintegrated at 158°C. The purchasers lost in a claim under this Act of 1979. This was simply because the purpose for which the goods were required was not made known to the sellers, who were able to satisfy the Courts that their normal method of production and packing was suitable for normal needs.[3] The Act requires goods to be of merchantable quality. This means, says section 14, 'as fit for the pur-

pose for which goods of that kind are commonly bought as it is reasonable to expect, having regard to any description applied to them, the price (if relevant) and all the other relevant circumstances'.

This case shows clearly how important it is to let a supplier or seller know the particular purpose of the purchase of the goods, especially if it is slightly abnormal.

We turn therefore to the Act and summarise its main provisions. These may be conveniently grouped in relation to subject matter and contract formation; conditions and warranties including title to the goods; performance; and breach. The earlier account in this chapter of normal contract principles will reduce the need for repetitive explanations.

Subject matter and contract formation

'Goods' are not defined; as saleable and moveable property, they can be distinguished on the one hand from fixed property such as houses and land and, on the other, from services. It was the combined provision of goods and services, such as a domestic washer plus a maintenance contract, which, in the Courts, took such contracts out of the Sale of Goods Act and led to the need for further legislation. This said, there is still a multitude of items of goods alone, which are dealt with under this Act.

Simply as a matter of definition, the Act of 1979 defines a contract for the sale of goods as one in which the seller transfers or agrees to transfer, the property (ie the legal term sometimes used for ownership) in goods to the buyer for a price, ie the money consideration.

The contract may be in writing or by word of mouth. It may be partly in one form and partly in the other. It may indeed be by conduct.

The goods may exist when the contract is made. If they are to come into existence after that date, they are referred to as 'future goods'.

The goods may, unknown to the parties, have perished at the time of the agreement, as might have happened if those Kuwait plastic cans of chemical had been sold to a third party, in the innocent belief that the contents were safe and sound. When goods are not in existence, in such circumstances, the contract is deemed void. It has the same effect if the goods perish before the property in them passes under the contract.

Occasionally the price is not fixed at the time of the contract; the Act simply states that it must be 'reasonable'.[4]

Conditions and warranties

We have given above the basic definitions; some of the interesting features of this Act, as shown in the Wormell Case, are the detailed terms which it imports into a contract, which has been silent on the points in question.

Implied conditions

1 That the seller has a right to sell the present goods and will have such a right in relation to future goods (section 12).
2 That the goods will correspond to the description of them in the contract.
3 That the goods are of merchantable quality, when sold in the course of business as defined above (section 14).[5]

4 That if the sale is by sample, the bulk will correspond with the sample, the buyer will have a reasonable opportunity to compare the bulk with the sample and the goods are such that such an examination will reveal any defect of a nature that would render the goods unmerchantable.

Implied warranties

1 That the goods are free from any undisclosed legal fetter, such as a charge in favour of a third party.
2 That the buyer will be able to enjoy undisturbed quiet possession of the goods.

Comment　Conditions and warranties are frequently the subject of argument between the parties to a contract and deserve care and attention when the contract is made.

Usage　Usage may be relied upon to imply a condition or warranty into a contract – apart from the above statutory ones – when it was not written down. For instance, in purchasing an extra diving board for a swimming pool, the limits of tension it should bear according to average and accepted weights of swimmers may be well established in the leisure field. Again the range of ambient and water temperatures may be sufficiently established to be called in aid in an argument about the materials to be used by an architect in a building which is to be subject to those temperatures.

Time　When parties wish time to be critical in relation to the performance of the contract, then they must say so. This is traditionally expressed as: 'time is deemed to be of the essence in this matter' (section 10).

A buyer may always waive a condition; likewise he may elect to treat a condition (breach of which would allow rejection of the contract and recovery of the price paid) as a warranty (breach of which would only give rise to a claim for damages resulting from that breach).

Performance

When the property passes　There are rules in the Act of 1979 about the time when the property and therefore the risk if it is lost or stolen, passes from the seller to the buyer. Like a lot of legal rules, they become critical only when things go wrong:

1 The property does not pass until the goods are ascertained; this could happen for a large contract of, for example, turf, for a new playing field when part of a larger quantity is allocated by the seller to the contract in question.
2 The property passes normally when the parties so intend, eg if it should be in the possession of the buyer on a sale or return basis, when he notifies the seller that he will buy.
3 Even if the buyer has the possession of the goods, the seller may have to fulfil a condition and tell the buyer he has done so, before the ownership will pass in law.

Title – open market sales　A defective title by the seller will cause problems. This is a complex area where we cannot go into detail. Fraud and deceit, as in the classic case of tampered odometers in car sales, can give rise to a sale to a bamboozled purchaser who wants his money back. We have discussed misrepresentation, mistake and frustration earlier in the section on contract and will not repeat those points here. The law seeks to balance the rights of what are sometimes two innocent parties – one being a purchaser who in good faith parted with money for some goods which were not what he thought he was getting and the other an innocent sub-seller who did not know that the consignment of, perhaps, sports equipment, was stolen property, or maybe under a charge to a manufacturer or otherwise that he really had no good legal title to pass on.

The Act of 1979 (section 22) does provide one guide line, namely that a good title can be passed when sale occurs in open market to a purchaser who acts in good faith and without knowledge of the defect or want of title in the seller.

Delivery   Delivery may cause problems. The seller should normally deliver the goods (section 27) but the parties can agree to vary this basic rule. It could, for instance, be agreed that delivery to the carrier was good legal delivery to the buyer.

On the other hand, the buyer must accept delivery and, if he refuses, the seller can hold him responsible for any deterioration in the goods (section 37).

If the circumstances show that the buyer is not acting reasonably, the seller can treat him as rejecting the contract and then sue the buyer for consequential damages.

If the wrong quantities are delivered, the buyer must decide whether or not to accept, in which case the contract rate will normally apply to the altered quantity.

The last snag may be that the money has not been paid when it should be. In this situation the Act gives the seller three rights:

1 He has a lien on the goods, ie a right to possess them until he is paid.
2 If the buyer becomes insolvent, the seller can stop the goods, in transit if necessary.
3 He can notify the buyer, and then re-sell the goods, recovering any loss from the buyer.

Breach of contract

1 If the property passes but no payment is made, the seller may sue for the price.
2 If the buyer refuses to accept, he may be sued for damages. These will be the estimated loss naturally and directly resulting from the breach. This may well be the difference between the contract price and the market price at that point in time.
3 The buyer can also exercise a right to sue, if the seller does not deliver as agreed.
4 If the very goods – and no substitute – are important, then a party can go to Court for an Order of Specific Performance, to make the reluctant party perform the contract. This would be an alternative to damages.
5 Breach of warranty, as mentioned above, can also give rise to an action for damages.

All in all, the subject is complex and the pattern of the Act is to take the parties through the whole transaction, spelling out rights and duties at each stage.

Notes

1 *Wormell v RHM Agricultural (East) Ltd* (1986) 1 WLR 336.
2 The others deal with consumer safety, adequate trade descriptions and consumer credit, to mention but three aspects.
3 *M/S Aswan Engineering Establishment Co v Lupdine Ltd and others* (1986) *The Times* 4 August 1986.
4 There are other Acts which provide procedures to settle prices in certain commercial situations, such as the Resale Prices Act 1976 and the Consumer Credit Act 1974.
5 The condition about merchantable quality does not apply if the buyer has had defects drawn to his attention or, secondly, if he has inspected the goods himself and defects are such that inspection should have revealed them (section 14).

5.7 Company formation

A company duly limited under this country's Companies Acts requires certain legal components. These include a board of directors, a secretary, a memorandum of association, articles of association, a stated share capital and a registered office. The short explanation given here of the formation of such a company will attempt little more than a clarification of some of these technical terms.

Directors

The articles of association will state the number of directors the company is to have. It will, for a private company, usually be a small number. One will normally be appointed managing director. Both the board and the managing director will operate from day to day under stated delegated powers. The board's powers will be set out in the articles and the managing director's powers will be decided by the board.[1]

The directors are responsible to the registrar under the Companies Acts for managing the company in accordance with the law. They are also responsible to meetings of shareholders for running the company in accordance with the wishes and policy approved by the shareholders. These meetings will be the annual one required by law and can also be extraordinary general meetings, which would be used only where speed was essential for a decision. The majorities needed for decisions vary depending on whether they require ordinary, extraordinary or special resolutions.

The directors will normally have substantial shareholdings themselves. A register at the companies office, available to shareholders, must show particulars of the directors. A register at the same office must also show shareholdings of the directors in the company. The general meeting has powers to remove directors.

Directors must avoid a conflict of interest in the course of their duties. They are also under a legal duty of good faith to the company.

Memorandum and articles of association

The memorandum of association is an important document. It sets out the name and objects of the company. It also states its registered office and the amount of capital with which it is to be registered. Whilst that is its nominal capital, the nominal value is shown by the number of shares actually being issued and their value. Quite often the value at this stage will be £1 a share.

Two members are sufficient in law to sign and certify the facts in the memorandum and proceed to form a company.

The articles of association is the document which describes how the company is managed. It may be taken from a model in the Companies Act. This document is where the rights of shareholders are set out and also the powers of directors. The details affecting shareholders' meetings will also be found here.

Formation
This description of the legal framework of a limited liability company provides the background to our noting that, to form such a company, there must be submitted to the Registrar of Companies:

1 The memorandum of association.
2 The articles of association.
3 A statement of the nominal value of the company.
4 A statement of the names of the directors, secretary and the registered office.
5 A statutory declaration that the requirements of the Companies Act have been complied with.

In practice these can go to a company agent firm in London, who will attend to the registration and pay the fee.[2]

Comment
This short account of the mechanics of limited company formation would not be complete without some comment on the legal implications for the company.

Section 9 provides that, in favour of the person dealing with a company in good faith, both the company and the directors shall be deemed freed of any limitation placed upon their powers by the articles of association.[3]

This is a major reform but we emphasise that it is a benefit only to customers. They are not to suffer because the company exceeded its powers. But it does not relieve a limited liability company of so managing its affairs that it acts within the articles of association: the company itself could be penalised if it exceeds those powers.

Notes

1 The minimum number of directors is two, unless the company was registered before 1929, when one will suffice, or it is a private company.
2 It may bring some of this to earth to mention that the agent's charge for forming a company currently is of the order of £125.
3 Under the Companies Act 1980 where the present law is gathered.

5.8 Value added tax

Value Added Tax (VAT) was introduced into this country in 1973 as part of the European Community fiscal machinery, succeeding Purchase Tax which had been in force since the 1940s. Originally 10 per cent, it has been levied at 15 per cent since 1979.

It is imposed on:

1 Import of goods into the UK.
2 Supply of goods and services in the UK.
3 In certain circumstances, the import of services by a business.

Practice

A return to Customs and Excise by each relevant business is required at the end of each accounting period (usually three months). This relates to its supplies and services.

Within a month the business has to account for VAT included in its sales and services income (ie 'outputs' as they are called). Expenditure incurred by the business which includes VAT (or 'inputs') is balanced against 'outputs' and the differences accounted for to Customs and Excise (or refunded by that Department if 'inputs' exceed 'outputs').

So the business does not actually suffer any tax but acts as a 'collector of tax'. That is why VAT is called a sales tax. The system is completed by penalties for overdue returns, zero rating for exports, food and many other items sold in the UK, as well as certain exemptions not relevant to the public leisure services.[1] VAT tribunals deal with appeals against Customs and Excise decisions. VAT inspectors have powers to inspect the books and records of a business, to ensure that accurate returns are being made.

Application

It is the 'business' which is the accountable unit; this term is sufficiently widely defined to include sports clubs and members' clubs. So, for instance, admission fees of the National Trust are VAT taxable as a business.

There is at present a threshold of £22,100 in respect of taxable supplies. There is also a method by which a business may become de-registered.

The business activities of local authorities are treated in the normal way but input tax on non-business activities, like social services, is refunded.

Note

1 Notices from Customs and Excise VAT offices show seventeen zero rated items, including caravans and eleven exempted items, including betting, gaming and lotteries. There are twenty notices, each about its own special topic. There are also helpful booklets obtainable from the local VAT office. It was the Finance Act 1972 which introduced VAT and most subsequent Finance Acts have had a reference to the subject.

6 Licensing and Gambling

Each of these areas of law has an airing in Parliament on an almost annual basis to keep pace with changing habits, technical ingenuity and fads in our society. Licensing hours were extended in 1987 to permit the extended lunch service; bingo habits gave rise to a special Act on that pastime in 1985.

In this chapter we shall survey the main topics in licensing law, ie the controls on premises, hours and licences, the restrictions affecting clubs and young persons and also the main offences. In relation to gambling, we shall limit our consideration to those areas of the subject most likely to be met by those in the public/leisure services. These are bingo, gaming machines, clubs and lotteries.

6.1 Licensing

Many branches of our law use licences as the name for legal permits, such as fishing, erecting an advertisement hoarding or, as issued by local authorities, the provision of entertainment. It is, however, the law about the supply and sale of intoxicating liquor which, as a matter of history, has acquired the grand title of licensing law. Presumably it was the first in the field for understandable reasons. Our present law is complex and we consider it now topic by topic.

Licences

There are eight types of permission and all are obtained from the local licensing justices.[1]

The **on licence** is for the sale of intoxicating liquor to be consumed on or off the premises and is needed by the traditional public house. It authorises a named person to carry on this business at named premises. It may relate to all descriptions of drinks or be limited either to beer, cider and wine, possibly beer and cider or even wine and nothing else, ie the wine bar.

The **off licence** is for the sale by a named person at named premises of drinks to be consumed off those premises. This is the licence needed by the whole range of shops from village store to the latest supermarket. It will be for all drinks or for beer, cider and wine only.

A **transfer** is the approval to the transfer of an on or off licence to another person for business at the same premises. It allows licensing justices an opportunity to satisfy themselves that the new holder is a suitable person.

A **removal**, on the other hand, is the consent needed when the holder of a licence at one set of premises wishes to take that licence with him to other premises.

A **provisional licence** is obtainable when it is intended to retail liquor from premises not currently licensed for that purpose. This could be if those premises were being newly built or being created by alteration or by extension of the existing premises. The provisional licence is a measure of approval by the licensing justices on the basis of building plans shown to them.

A **table licence** is obtained for premises bona fide used to provide a customary main meal at midday or in the evening or both for customers and the liquor is *ancillary* to those meals.

A **residential licence** is used for the premises where board and lodging are provided habitually. One of the main meals, including breakfast, must be customary. Then the supply or sale must be limited to residents or their bona fide friends. It can be combined with a restaurant licence if appropriate.

An **occasional licence** is used for multifarious dances, dinners, fêtes and galas when a one-off function often includes the sale of liquor. It is taken out from the justices by the supplier of the liquor or someone on his behalf. It could be the promoter of the event; with his name on the licence he becomes responsible to the licensing justices for due compliance with the law at the function in question. There are a number of details relating to these licences which should be noted:

1 The police normally require 24 hours notice of the application.
2 They cannot authorise sales on public holidays nor Christmas Day and Good Friday.
3 Wales and Monmouth are outside this procedure.[2]
4 A public hearing is avoided if one month's notice of the application is duly given to the clerk of the justices.
5 The name of the licence holder needs to be displayed at the place where the function is held.
6 A recent statute, the Licensing (Occasional Permissions) Act 1983, is designed to simplify the grant of occasional licences by giving them a new name and allowing an officer 'of an eligible organisation' to apply. The organisations in question are those not conducted for private gain. The 1983 Act stipulates that such 'occasional permissions' are not to be more than four per annum. Each one is given for 24 hours only, so that each of, say, the four requires a separate permission. These applications, though conceived as a simpler procedure, can still attract objections.[3]

Duration
As with the last instance, so all these licences are limited in duration. The on and off licences require annual renewal at the licensing sessions, which are timed to fit in with the licensing year from 6 April to the next 5 April. The occasional and provisional licences clearly have a built-in termination date.

When a new on or off licence is granted in the last three months of a licensing year the period will run to the end of the subsequent licensing year.

Obtaining licences
The justices are to be satisfied that they have a named and accountable individual as the licensee and that he or she is a fit and proper person for that job. The licensee is normally the person who will be selling the liquor. With a company or corporation it is clearly an employee but it could be the hall manager or catering director. Previous convictions are a disqualifying feature;[4] the Crown Courts hear appeals from justices' decisions in these matters.

Permitted hours

This area of licensing law was scrutinised by Parliament at the time of the extension of luncheon sales times, dealt with in the Licensing (Restaurant Meals) Act 1987. The present rules are:

1 For licensed premises, 11 am to 10.30 pm with a break of $2^{1}/_{2}$ hours which begins at 3 pm.
2 The afternoon break is not now necessary when the sales are ancillary to a meal.
3 The 10.30 pm closing time is extended to 11 pm in the Metropolitan District and elsewhere when the licensing justices so agree.
4 On Christmas Day, Good Friday and Sundays, the permitted hours are 12 noon to 10.30 pm, with a 5 hour afternoon break, commencing at 2 pm.
5 When licensing justices agree, perhaps for a sporting event or other local jollification, they can modify these general licensing hours. The normal $9^{1}/_{2}$ hour opening can become 10 or $10^{1}/_{2}$ hours, by opening at 10 am and limiting the afternoon break to 2 hours.
6 Traditionally and legally, a 20 minute drinking up time is allowed at the end of these various sessions.
7 A resident at the licensed premises and his bona fide guests are not subject to these restraints.
8 The standard permitted hours can be varied by the justices to cover the provision of refreshment or entertainment or both.
9 Finally, if the premises have an entertainment licence from the local authority under the Local Government (Miscellaneous Provisions) Act 1982, the licensing justices can grant a special hours certificate so that the licensing hours coincide with those in the entertainment licence.

Inspections and alterations

Before its first registration or licence, the premises will be inspected for fitness for their purpose. The police, the fire authority and also the local authority have a right to inspect at this time.[5]

Alterations to licensed premises are checked before approval. The circumstances of special interest to licensing justices are when the effect of the works would be to increase the drinking facilities in the public or common parts of the premises; again, the works might conceal from observation a public or common part of the premises used for drinking or these works might affect the means of communication between the bar area and the rest of the premises or, indeed, with adjacent streets; in these cases also the authorities will inspect before consent to the proposed alterations is given.[6]

Young persons

Licensing law is slightly complex in its current provisions touching on the age of young persons and facilities at licensed premises:

1 An under 14 year old must not be in a bar during opening hours.[7] There is an exception for a child of the licence holder and also for a resident.
2 A 16 year old may buy beer, cider, porter or perry, to accompany a meal in the part of the premises set aside for that purpose.
3 An under 18 year old must not consume liquor in a bar nor must liquor be sold to him.[7]
4 It is an offence also for the licensee to employ a person under 18 years old in a bar during opening hours.

Clubs

The permitted hours for sales of liquor are fixed by the club management. However these hours must not begin earlier nor end later than the times fixed under the general licensing law in that district. The afternoon break must be at least two hours.

A restriction affects clubs in relation to Sundays, Christmas Day and Good Friday. This is that permitted hours on those days must not exceed $3^1/2$ hours after 5 pm and the hours of 3 pm to 5 pm shall be part of the afternoon break.[8]

Offences

Numerous offences are created under the Act of 1968. Indeed, as an example of the proliferation of offences under this branch of the law, when an occasional licence is being operated, it has been calculated that the licence holder is in peril of committing no less than fourteen different offences. Of course the most obvious and main perils of coming into conflict with the law relate to selling or supplying liquor during non-permitted hours, aiding and abetting consumption during those hours, selling from unlicensed premises, or supplying liquor to persons who are not bona fide guests of the resident. These are but instances of the range of this aspect of licensing law. Fines and imprisonment are the sanctions for most of these offences but occasionally the licence itself is in jeopardy, whether it be for a club, a public house, a retail shop or other premises.

Notes

1 Licensing Act 1964 section 2. This is our current major statute on this subject.

2 Unless an electors poll has produced a majority to adopt this part of the law.
3 See *R v Bromley Licensing Justices ex.p. Bromley Licensed Victuallers Association* (1984) 1 AER 794.
4 Act of 1964 section 9.
5 Act of 1964 schedule I.
6 Act of 1964 section 169.
7 Act of 1964 section 169. A bar set aside to serve table meal customers is not caught by this restriction, section 170.
8 Act of 1964 section 62.

6.2 Gambling

We use this title since *gaming* is the word for a specialised form of gambling. It is 'the playing of a game of chance for winnings in money or money's worth, whether any person playing the game is at risk of losing any money or money's worth or not'.[1] So gambling is the umbrella term for games, activities, machines which allow people, as a pastime or recreation, to engage in transactions in which money is won or lost on the happening of an event, the outcome of which is uncertain. The policy of Parliament has been to intervene only as necessary to regulate some form of gambling, which has reached a stage of social popularity to make legal guidelines desirable.

It may be noted that the police and fire authorities have powers of inspection of premises licensed under the Gaming Act 1968. Gaming Act inspectors also have powers of entry. Local authorities may not maintain nor contribute to the maintenance of premises with a Gaming Act licence. Lastly, there is a code of regulation about advertisements in connection with public gaming.[2]

Bingo

There are special rules for Bingo, which distinguish it from other forms of gaming at clubs.

1 A maximum limit is fixed for aggregate winnings in a week.
2 Persons under 18 may not play, though they may be present.
3 If games of bingo in several premises are played simultaneously they are treated as one game, ie linked bingo. The conditions for this to apply are that:
    a Winnings in aggregate are not more than stakes in aggregate.[3]
    b Winnings per week are kept within limits fixed by the Home Secretary.
    c The condition of a 48 hour waiting period between application and acceptance for club membership is reduced to 24 hours.
4 There is an excise duty, called bingo duty, which is described in detail in sections 17–20 in the Betting and Gaming Duties Act 1981.

Gaming machines

A legal code about this subject is contained in Part III of the Gaming Act 1968 and may be summarised:

1 It is an offence to practise gaming by machines except in accordance with the conditions in this Act.[4]
2 Linked offences are created for supplying, selling and maintaining gaming machines for use on unlicensed premises.
3 The permitted exemptions are numerous, viz:
    a If the persons and premises have respectively certificates and permits from the Gaming Board and the premises are:
       i a pleasure pier, or
       ii a travelling showman's fair, or
       iii a pleasure fair devoted mainly to amusements, or
       iv where the machines are to be used on premises which are wholly or mainly for amusements by means of these machines.
    b If the premises in question are a members club or a miners welfare insti-

tute and are registered under Part II or III of the Act of 1968. But conditions in these circumstances are stringent, ie only two permitted machines, limits on prizes as well as on the charges for playing and on the minimum percentage of the total charges which must be paid out as prizes. Additionally the machines have to display a statement of the above amounts and, lastly, the public must not be allowed access when the machines are in use.

c Where the machines are incidental to non-commercial entertainment.

d Where the machines are primarily for amusement and the amount of the prizes is limited. Under a local authority permit, such fruit machines or one armed bandits may be set up at dinners, dances, sporting and athletic events and similar entertainments and extend more than one day. But apart from deducting expenses, the whole of the proceeds must go as prizes. Also the opportunity to win prizes must not be the only or only substantial inducement to people to attend the event.[5]

e Again the limit on machines to two applies in certain circumstances.

f Money may be removed from the machines by management only by authorised persons.

g The accounts, records and verification can be inspected by police and by the Gaming Board.

h Offences against these provisions can be met with fines or imprisonment.[6]

Clubs

A members club may be formed and there are rules to be met:

1 The club is to be registered with the local licensing justices. Notice of the application has to be given to the police, and to the customs and excise authorities. A similar requirement affects the formation of a miners welfare institute.

2 Grounds for refusing the application include:

a it has a bad record;

b it has less than 25 members, is temporary in character and is not a bona fide members club;

c if gaming appears to be the main purpose of the club, subject to an exemption on this item in favour of bridge and whist clubs.

3 The conditions imposed by the licensing authority may include a limitation on gaming to a defined part of the club premises.

4 The Crown Courts will hear appeals against refusals or conditions alleged to be unduly onerous.

5 Mismanagement of the club may provoke some citizen to invoke a procedure to have the licence cancelled. This provides for a hearing before the licensing justices, with both sides calling evidence and, as statutory backcloth, no less than eleven reasons which would justify cancellation.[7]

6 Registration, as the above implies, is short term and renewal allows for a check on performance. The period of registration may legally be for one year or some period up to ten years. Registration fees are payable.

Lotteries

The Lotteries and Amusements Act 1976 declares lotteries unlawful and then lists four exemptions. (A lottery is the distribution of prizes by lot or chance.) These bring local authorities into the licensing system, which may be described as follows:

Small lotteries incidental to entertainments is the expression used to cover bazaars, dances and sporting or other recreational events. There are rules about the prizes, the expenses and also about limits on the extent of selling tickets.

Private lotteries are those limited to members of a society or to people who live together or work together. There are twelve conditions to be met, all designed to ensure that the character of the lottery, as stated above, is not violated.

Societies' lotteries may be thought of as the charitable ones, since the purposes must be athletic sports or games or cultural activities or more than one of those purposes. The society promoting the lottery must be established for purposes which are not commercial nor for private gain. Registration with the local authority is necessary; if the total value of the tickets is higher than a prescribed limit, it must register also with the Gaming Board.

Local lotteries are the money raising ones which local authorities may themselves promote. They have to be within a scheme, approved by both the authority and the Gaming Board. The purpose to which the proceeds are to be devoted has, naturally, to be within the legal powers of the authority. A lottery fund has to be set up in which proceeds are kept, together with interest on that money. Decisions have to be taken by the full Council. Lastly, there are not to be more than 52 lotteries in a twelve month period. Offences are committed by breaching these conditions.

Notes

1 Gaming Act 1968 section 52. The dictionary makes it shorter: 'Gambling on games of chance'.
2 Ibid section 42. A broad prohibition is followed by carefully defined and limited permissions for specific activities. It merits study.
3 See Gaming Act 1968 section 20. The current limit was raised to £3000 recently. The Act of 1980 gave the Home Secretary power to vary this figure and this is done periodically. Also, the word 'bingo' is defined in the Statute to cover any variant by whatever name it is called.
4 Gaming Act 1968 section 38.
5 Lotteries and Amusements Act of 1976 section 15. As may be imagined, the word 'proceeds' has been litigated.
6 Ibid section 38.
7 See Gaming Act 1968 schedule III para 14.

7 Charities and trusts

A trust is an invention of English law which has developed enormously in this century. It exists where property is in the legal ownership of one person (the trustee) but that person is obliged in law to ensure that the benefit of that property is enjoyed by another person or persons (the beneficiaries). The trustee has the duty and the toil, the beneficiary has the benefit.

The trust has achieved this popularity because it is so useful. The golf club may own an extremely valuable course and club house, yet since membership fluctuates with a figure of perhaps more than a hundred, it would be clumsy in the extreme to make all the members 'owners'. So the land and buildings can be vested in say six trustees, no doubt officials of the club, but they are to be held for the benefit of all the members. The principle in this example has been applied in trusts for churches and chapels, working men's clubs, the managers of unit trusts, the disposition of property under a will and many more situations.[1] The advantages of the device are to allow a clear identification of the owners, a clear statement of their responsibilities, a flexibility in the numbers of beneficiaries and, not least, the knowledge that the Courts will enforce the arrangement.

Readers with a taste for legal history may enjoy unravelling the ways in which the arrangement which we call a trust has appeared and the dress it has worn since the Norman Conquest. That story will touch on the powerful influence of a Judge, Lord Nottingham, after the turbulence of the Civil War, in shaping the trust to become the respectable legal arrangement of our day.

Legal essentials

We may therefore now list the essentials of a valid trust.

Three certainties[2]

Because the trustee's duty is so critical, and is so different from that of the unfettered landowner, the law looks for certainty in:

1 the words creating the trust;

2 the property which is subject to the trust, and also
3 the objects or persons to benefit from the trust.

Over the years, the Courts have resolved many cases where some of these items were vague. For instance a gift to be used for the benefit of 'all the residents of London' would clearly be uncertain.[3] Other expressions which could be vague and thus render a trust void, could be 'old friends', 'customers of my company' and 'members of my family'.

Though the objects of the intended trust appear to be suitable, if they are vaguely expressed the trust will be void under this principle. Two recent examples are a provision for 'the week's good cause' (when it transpired that seven different good causes were advocated in one week by broadcasters from different radio stations)[4] and a desire to share an estate among 'worthy causes'.[5]

Writing

The manner of creating a trust is governed by statute only where a trust relates to land. The Law of Property Act 1925 (section 53) says that: 'A declaration of trust respecting any land or any interest therein must be manifested and proved by some writing signed by some person who is able to declare such trust or by his will.' Although writing is often useful in showing the intentions of persons creating a trust, it is not essential, except in this case of land.

The trust is completely constituted

Sometimes although the above conditions are fulfilled there is some hurdle to be cleared before the trustees can act as trustees. In law the situation is described as an incompletely constituted trust. The important practical defect which it creates is that a beneficiary will not be able to enforce his rights. Perhaps the settlor has not transferred every part of the property to the trustees or he has some other action to take. This is the type of situation that leaves a trust which is incomplete in law.

Private, public and charitable trusts

According to their purpose, trusts may be divided in these ways.

Private

A trust is private when it is for the benefit of an individual or class of individuals, even though some benefit may be conferred on the public at large. A benefactor might create a trust for the training of swimmers between the ages of 8 and 10 who lived in some suburb of Hemel Hempstead, where he also lived. This would seem to be a sufficiently small and ascertainable class of beneficiaries that it could be viable but it would be private, within the above definition. The objects would have to be certain and the way in which the benefits were to be enjoyed would also have to be clear. It could be managed via the local swimming club and would, additionally, have to avoid the rule against perpetuities.[6]

Public

A trust is public when the object is the public welfare, even though, incidentally, an individual or class may benefit. Since many charitable trusts also serve the public welfare, we have to have some way of separating the two classes. We shall set out below the definition of a charitable trust; at this point, it may help to think of trusts which require political action for their attainment as a prime example of a public trust which is not charitable. Thus the Anti Vivisection Society would seem to require legislation for their objects to be achieved and thus be a public trust, as the Courts have held.[7] In another case the objects of Amnesty International were scrutinised in the Courts and held not to be for the public welfare, on the ground that they involved reversing the views of a foreign government.[8]

Charitable

A charitable trust is one which is for the public welfare but also comes within one of four historic classes. These are for the advancement of education; for the advancement of religion; the relief of poverty; and 'other charitable purposes'. These expressions go back to a leading case of 1891 and statute of 1601[9] and each has been scrutinised by the Courts on numerous occasions. Sports prizes have been held to be within the first class; a disaster fund has been held to be within the last class.

Sport as such is not 'charitable' but can be if ancillary to some larger, charitable objective, like education. So the cases show a contrast between a trust purely to advance yacht racing (not charitable)[10] and one to promote 'association football or other games or sports' by pupils at schools and universities for the purpose of promoting their physical and mental development (charitable).[11]

Things that go wrong

Trustees can commit breaches of trust

The Trustee Act 1925 (section 61) states that a trustee may be relieved by the Court of liability for breach of trust if he has acted honestly, reasonably, and ought fairly to be excused. The Courts look for all three of these conditions to be met. Examples of circumstances when a trustee might not come within section 61 could be where he failed to keep the trust property under review, allowing it to deteriorate and thereby lose value; or recklessly paid trust funds to a fraudulent applicant; or did not recover trust funds zealously; or made ill-advised investments of trust funds.

Void trusts

If a trust infringes the law or violates public policy it is absolutely void. A clear case was where trustees placed trust money with a company in order to allow it to give the appearance of being in credit, whilst the company directors had an understanding with the trustees that the money would be used only for trust purposes.[12]

Impaired trusts

The trust may suffer because of mistake, fraud, duress or undue influence – the same group of baleful matters which imperil contracts. The problems created by these unacceptable elements can be sorted out by the Courts. The circumstances giving rise to these situations have often been domestic, such as marriage, divorce or arrangements for children, occasionally about patients and their medical advisers. The public leisure services seem, so far, to have remained free of these taints.

Notes

1   We may refer to settlements and settlors in due course and thus explain that a settlement is the legal arrangement by which property is arranged to pass to different persons in succession eg to children on the death of a surviving parent. A settlor is the creator of a settlement.
2   Lord Langdale in 1840. *Knight v Knight* (1840) 52 RR 74.
3   *McPhail v Doulton* (1971) AC 424.
4   Re Wood (1949) Ch 498.
5   Re Atkinson's Will Trusts (1978) 1 AER 1275.
6   A complex subject. Twenty-one years is the period to follow, in the absence of other information and guidance in the instrument creating the trust.
7   *National Anti Vivisection Society v I.R.C.* (1948) AC 31.
8   *McGovern v A–G* (1982).
9   The case is *The Commissioners of Income Tax v Pemsel* (1891) AC 583 and the statute is the Statute of Charitable Uses.
10 Re Nottage (1895) 2 Ch 649.
11 Re Mariette (1915) 2 Ch 284.
12 Re Great Berlin Steamboat Co. (1884) 26 ChD 616.

8 Areas of liaison

It is essential for managers in the leisure services to be aware of their aids and allies. A grant from the Sports Council at the right time can tip the balance for an important scheme. Support from a National Park Planning Board or Committee with the government can make or break a development dear to the heart of a community and its local authority.

So each of the seven bodies described in this chapter is responsible for some activity the leisure service manager will meet. He will doubtless build his own lines of communication with them, for liaison, especially in a crisis, can be vital.

8.1 The Forestry Commission

The role of the Forestry Commission in relation to the public leisure services is seen best by a glance at its statutory 'charter', section 23 of the Countryside Act 1968, 'The Commission may, on any land placed at their disposal by the Minister of Agriculture, Fisheries and Food or the Secretary of State for Wales, provide or arrange for or assist in the provision of, tourist, recreational or sporting facilities and any equipment, facilities and works ancillary thereto.' This gave rise to the gradual development of the following facilities:

1 Accommodation for visitors.
2 Information and display centres.
3 Camping and caravan sites.
4 Public conveniences and places for meals and refreshments.
5 Picnic places, viewing sites, routes for nature study and footpaths for walkers.
6 Parking places and shops to support some the above facilities.

The supporting byelaws made by the Commission seek to regulate the conduct of visitors to the land holdings of some two million acres. The legislative guidelines for those byelaws are in the Forestry Act 1967, section 46. This authorises byelaws which are designed to prohibit and regulate anything tending to the injury and disfigurement of the land or its amenities. Additionally, the byelaws can regulate 'the reasonable use of the land by the public for the purposes of exercise and recreation'. The Commission updates its byelaws as visitors present new problems. Subjects recently covered include metal detectors, beehives and hot air balloons.

The Commission look upon prosecutions and fines under their byelaws as a last sanction. They therefore publicise their Forest Code, which sets out detailed reasonable standards which they invite visitors to accept when using the Commission's land and facilities.

The Commission is best known, perhaps, for its tree planting and felling activities, indeed everything associated with afforestation. This stems legally from the Forestry Act 1967, which is the current parent Act and contains the constitution and powers of the Commission.[1] These permit the Commission to plant trees, not only as part of an afforestation but also 'in the interests of amenity' (*see* Countryside Act 1968 section 24).

The Ministers to whom the Commission is responsible are the Minister of Agriculture, Fisheries and Food in England, and the Secretaries of State for England and Wales. In this instance, the Secretary of State for Scotland acts as the senior minister.

The most recent statutes touching on the Commission were the Forestry Act 1979, which dealt with metrification, loans and grants, the Forestry Act 1981, which covered disposals of land, and the Wild Creatures and Forest Laws Act 1971 about Royal rights in forests.

The Forestry Commission is only too anxious to liaise with those in the public services about matters of mutual interest.

Note

1 The Commission began its life under an Act of 1919 but that first Act and others were repealed and consolidated in the Act of 1967.

8.2 The National Trust

Every manager in the public leisure services will have dealings with the National Trust at some time. The Trust is owner of large numbers of stately homes and monuments as well as holding a vast portfolio of landholdings, not least on the coast and in the National Parks. Its 1987 annual report boasts of 8.5m visitors to its properties. The autumn hurricane in that year destroyed no less than 250,000 trees of the Trust.

The Trust operates under Acts of Parliament and we now summarise the legal framework they provide, so that those dealing with them are aware of these constraints.

Purposes

Originally set out in the National Trust Act 1907, and later extended, the Trust's purposes are to:

> Promote the permanent preservation, for the benefit of the nation, of lands and tenements (including buildings) of beauty or historic interest and, as regards lands, for the preservation (so far as practicable) of their natural aspect, features, and animal and plant life.

The reference to buildings was later strengthened to describe those of national, architectural, historical or artistic interest. The amenities of the building were also included.

The contents were then specifically mentioned, as was the aspect of public enjoyment of these buildings.

The Trust's general powers for acquiring and managing land and buildings support these purposes.

Additionally, the Trust is empowered to keep open common land, do what is necessary in the interests of good estate management, and set parts of the lands apart for games, meetings and sports gatherings.

The Trust is then authorised to make byelaws to regulate the use of these properties, to secure their protection, to preserve order and to control visitors.

Non-disposable assets

The Trust owns a number of properties which they have no power to dispose of, such as the Admiral Hardy monument in Dorset and the Ruskin monument in Keswick. The Trust has power to add to these properties (National Trust Act 1971 section 28). This feature does not prevent the Trust from granting leases of these properties.

Public leisure service managers may be employed by authorities which are tempted to try to acquire National Trust lands for allotments or to add to National Parks but such acquisitions, by compulsory purchase, are precluded by Acts of Parliament, which protect the Trust.

Restrictions on development

There is one last notable legal feature of Trust land, found in the National Trust Act 1971 (section 27). The general law allows Courts to modify or remove restrictive covenants imposed on land where those restrictions have become outdated due to changes in the character of the neighbourhood. The Trust is in the special position that such legal flexibility is not to apply to Trust properties, where restrictions exist to preserve or protect its amenities or to secure access or enjoyment by the public. It would normally be to facilitate property development that the Courts would be asked to change restrictive covenants about building, or perhaps building to a particular density; the protection of the Trust from such approaches is a singular mark of the esteem in which the Trust is held as custodian of important properties.

8.3 The Sports Council

We are concerned here only with the legal framework within which the Sports Council works. Its general policies and nationwide promotions will be considered in other books in the Longman/ILAM Leisure Management Series.

Aims

The Council was created by Royal Charter as recently as 1972. This laid down that its main objects should be 'fostering the knowledge and practice of sport and physical education among the public at large and the provision of facilities therefor'. Additionally the Charter requires the Council 'to encourage the attainment of high standards in conjunction with the governing bodies of sport and physical education'.

These broad objects have been sufficient to allow the Sports Council to engage in dialogue with the representatives of as many as 50 different sports in this country. In addition, the Council has assisted them with grant schemes in the improvement of their facilities and has itself set up centres of excellence, thus helping to promote the highest standards.

Grants

A recent annual report shows the main divisions of the financial support given, namely:

1 Grant aid to governing bodies of sport for administration, coaching and competitions amounting to £13.7m. This took the form of granting about half to projects in individual sports and the other half to 25 organising bodies for sport in all its forms.
2 Capital expenditure of some £4m was divided into about £3m for the seven national centres run by the Council at Crystal Palace, Holme Pierrepont and elsewhere, and the balance to capital projects of the governing bodies of various sports.

3 Capital grants and loans to the total of £5.6m channelled through the nine regional centres.

All this represents a very busy organisation, seeking to spread its support where it is most needed.

The Council has set up nine regional Councils of Sport and Recreation. Their membership is representative of the sports associations and local authorities in the region in question. Their main functions are to foster the provision of sports facilities and the attainment of high standards in these sports.

This involves day to day liaison with the local authorities, who regularly submit schemes for grant aid to them. The Council distributes grants on the basis of their intrinsic merit and of each local authority's area, with the largest grants for schemes which serve a larger area, by straddling local authority boundaries.

The regional councils also make grants available to encourage the attendance of promising young sportmen at centres of excellence.

Additionally the Sports Council has ten panels of experts, so that it can try to keep abreast of needs and developments in key areas affecting sport in our society. Drug abuse, coaching and sports science are examples.

It may be noted that there is a separate Sports Council for Wales and Scotland.

Recently the Minister for Sport has announced his intention to reconstitute the Council to facilitate ease of decision-making. To this end the new Council will be severely reduced in size – membership being restricted to twelve to fourteen as compared with a previous membership of 32.

The Council recognises a continuing need to help the disabled to enjoy appropriate sporting facilities. It also promotes research in various fields.

The Charter has been found to be an adequate base from which to develop an enterprising organisation.

8.4 The National Parks and the Countryside Commission

During the last 40 years this country has seen the creation of National Parks in the Lake District, the Peak District, the Yorkshire Dales, Snowdonia, Dartmoor and elsewhere. These are large tracts of countryside to which the public are naturally attracted. The National Park status is designed to provide the legal machinery by which a balance is held between encouraging public and tourist enjoyment and conserving and preserving the natural amenities, so that they may be enjoyed by future generations.

There are five parties who are involved in this scene:

1 The group of voluntary societies which have grown in the last 100 years to keep a watchful eye on this whole scene. This first group may be referred to briefly and then we shall turn to the other four, each of which has statutory duties to perform.
2 The Countryside Commission, which creates and oversees National Parks.
3 The managing body, whether it be board or committee, for the park in question.

4 The local authorities in whose area the park lies.
5 The Nature Conservancy Council.

Voluntary Societies

1 The National Trust, as we have seen, came into existence at the turn of the century.
2 The Council for the Preservation of Rural England is the second body, whose title speaks for itself.
3 The Ramblers' Association has maintained a watchdog role over any moves by landowners or the authorities which threaten public footpaths. This inevitably makes them keenly interested in National Parks. The Association is notable for its readiness to marshal members from time to time to walk footpaths and thus demonstrate these rights when the paths are public rights of way.
4 Lastly, the Commons Preservation Society has a special interest.

These eminent societies are available for consultation on matters affecting their members' interests.

The Countryside Commission

This is the current name for the body set up in 1949 as the National Park Commission. (The name was amended when Country Parks and Areas of Outstanding Natural Beauty also came into being and the Commission's role was extended.)

It is a corporate body, whose chairman and members are appointed by the Secretary of State. It is responsible for England and Wales. A separate Commission deals with Scotland.

Main statutes

Its objects and powers are set out in the three major statutes which have charted the Parliamentary course through this scene, viz the National Parks and Access to the Countryside Act 1949, the Countryside Act 1968 and the Wildlife and Countryside Act 1981.

Commission's duties

The Commission's duties under these Acts are:

1 Preserve and enhance the natural beauty in England and Wales, especially in National Parks.
2 Encourage the provision or improvement of facilities for visitors to the National Parks.
3 Promote the enjoyment of the Parks and opportunities for open air recreation and the study of nature.

The Commission must render an annual report. It can charge for its services. It can accept gifts which assist its work. It has wide powers of acting to advance its functions.[1]

It is under a duty to confer with local planning authorities. It is also to advise and assist persons with proposals submitted to the Commission.

The Commission is authorised to provide publicity and information services which are seen in part in the information centres commonly found in our National Parks.

The Commission is empowered to engage in experimental schemes.

Lastly, the Commission can create long distance routes for travellers by foot, bicycle or horseback. These schemes involve detailed discussions with landowners and local authorities.[2]

Management of a National Park

National Parks were initially constituted under the National Parks and Access to the Countryside Act 1949. They are, said that Act, 'extensive tracts of country in England and Wales as to which it appears to the Commission that by reason of their natural beauty and the opportunities they afford for open air recreation, having regard both to their character and to their position in relation to centres of population, it is especially desirable that steps should be taken to promote their enjoyment by the public' (section 5). The procedure was for the Commission to designate them by Order and for the then minister to confirm the Order. (It is now the Secretary of State for the Environment who would do so.)

Currently there are nine viz the Peak District, the Lake District, Snowdonia, Dartmoor, Pembrokeshire Coast, North York Moors, Yorkshire Dales, Exmoor, Northumberland and the Brecon Beacons.

Administration
A National Park is not publicly owned, though it is publicly administered. The form of administration depends on whether or not its area falls completely within the area of one local authority or within the areas of a number of such bodies. Since the major local government reforms of 1974 altered local authorities and their boundaries, the present law about the administration of National Parks is to be found in the Local Government Act 1972 schedule 17.

The complex details need not detain us but the Lake District Special Planning Board is so called and empowered because it falls within the new county of Cumbria. On the other hand, the Peak District Joint Planning Board is 'joint' since more than one authority forms its area. Those two Boards exercise district and county planning functions.

The other seven National Parks are each administered by a National Park Committee. Such a body does not exercise detailed planning functions as in the Peak and Lake Districts above and those Committees are appointed by the county councils within whose areas the Park lies, or in default by the Secretary of State (Schedule 17 para 8).

The discharge of general planning functions in a National Park can be the subject of agreement between the National Park Committee, the Countryside Commission and the local authorities in question (ibid para 9).

Membership
Not less than a third of the members of a Special Planning Board, Joint Plan-

ning Board or National Park Committee are appointed by the Secretary of State (the proportion can be altered to a quarter in any particular case). The balance of members are appointed by the county councils in the case of a National Park Committee.

One of the legal duties laid upon the management of a National Park is the production of a National Park Plan. This formulates the policy in managing the Park; it is renewable every five years and is published.

Since 1981, local authorities whose areas fall within a National Park must publish and keep under review maps of the Park to show mountains, moors, heaths, cliffs and foreshore, whose natural beauty it is important to conserve. The Countryside Commission give guidance for this exercise (section 43 of the Wildlife and Countryside Act 1981).

Finally, the National Parks whether they are Committees or Boards liaise with local authorities. The local authorities for their part, under the Act of 1949 (section 12), may provide accommodation, refreshments, camping sites and car parks.

The National Park managers exercise a strategic role in making a National Park Plan which sets out the aims and programmes of development. These could relate to afforestation, the creation of public facilities, the improvement of footpaths and many other matters.

The Committees also exercise a more intimate management role. They appoint wardens, pay the bills, clear the litter, collect parking charges and negotiate the contracts. Wardens are expected to advise the public.

They also have power to make byelaws. These will be to regulate the conduct of visitors, protect special plants or wildlife features, probably regulate the use of water, whether lakes, streams or reservoirs, somewhat on the lines which we looked at earlier in this chapter for the Forestry Commission.

There are three classes of protective framework for our countryside. These are National Parks, as described, Country Parks and Areas of Outstanding Natural Beauty and we now describe the second and third of these.

Country Parks

Country Parks are created by local authorities to encourage the enjoyment of the countryside by the public. Local authorities are not restricted to their own area in devising the area of such a park (Countryside Act 1968 section 6). There has to be the fullest consultation before the final step is taken by such an authority and then the specific powers of a local authority in relation to a Country Park are:

1 To lay out, plant and improve the site, erect buildings and carry out works.
2 Provide facilities for the enjoyment of the public, including refreshments, car parks, shelters and conveniences.
3 Provide facilities for open air recreation.

The guidance given in Parliament when this new concept was being explained was that Clapham Common was less suitable for this designation than Box Hill in Surrey. The idea was clearly introduced in order to maintain the pace built up by the National Park programme by classifying as Country

Parks smaller areas that would still, as the Act says, serve 'an urban or built up' district.

Areas of Outstanding Natural Beauty

It is the Countryside Commission which can make orders designating these areas, of which examples are the Malvern Hills, the Forest of Bowland, Cannock Chase and the Wye Valley. There are legal powers to protect these areas in the Act of 1949 (sections 87 and 88) and byelaws and then access agreements will normally accompany designation. (Part V of the Act of 1949 has a virtual code of law about the creation of access agreements; of how special danger spots and woodlands are to be treated; about the compensation payable to landowners on to whose land the public will, by one of these agreements, be introduced. These details however go beyond the scope of this work.) It may be noted that Epping Forest and Burnham Beeches are outside this legal provision, since both come under the management of the City of London Authority (Act of 1949 section 112). It will be appreciated from the above that though the Countryside Commission is in no sense a local authority such bodies are intimately involved in the work of the Commission, first in so far as their members may be amongst those appointed by the Secretary of State to the Commission and then in conferring about the management and provision of facilities in these areas. Furthermore, the whole field of long distance highway routes is another example calling for the closest collaboration between local authorities and the Commission.

Local authorities

These bodies will have their representatives on the National Park Committee for their area and can be intimately involved if they accept an agency for some function of that Committee.

They may, as local planning authorities, set up study centres and other facilities to help the public to learn all about the National Park.[3]

If the sea or a waterway forms the boundary of a National Park, then the local planning authority can carry out works to facilitate the use of those waters; it can supplement such works with byelaws.

They can enhance enjoyment by the public by use of their extensive powers to make access agreements with landowners or, if agreement cannot be secured, then by the making of access orders, to allow public entry.[4]

Nature Conservancy Council

Constituted under the Nature Conservancy Act 1973, this Council is given special powers in relation to the maintenance and management of National Nature Reserves.

The Council is particularly concerned about flora, fauna, geological or physiographical features.

It produces an annual report and takes directions from the Secretary of State for the Environment.

A nature reserve is a legally designated area, where protection of these wild creatures and their habitat is deemed to justify that legal step. The Council may grant licences to suitable persons to study in the reserve, take photographs, take education classes or perhaps assist in the conservation work. The legal protection given to a reserve extends to creating offences for making false statements in order to obtain these entry licences.

The Council's work is within the framework of the Act of 1981, under which schedules are promulgated of wild animals, birds, and plants which are protected by law. The Council advises the Secretary of State of periodic amendments to be made to these schedules.[5]

The Council's role is supported by local authorities who have a duty of bringing to the public notice these forms of protection for birds, animals and plants and can themselves take proceedings for offences. The Council is bidden in law to take account of the needs of agriculture, forestry and the social and economic needs of the area when designating these nature reserves.[6] It will not be surprising to learn, in the light of the above, that nature reserves are excluded from those lands to which legal access may be created in National Parks.

Sites of Special Scientific Interest

A related ancillary aspect of this subject is the occasional creation of Sites of Special Scientific Interest (SSSI). Whilst the nature reserve consists primarily of land which is managed to support study and research into the elements mentioned above, the Sites of Special Scientific Interest are lands which, whilst not in the nature reserve, are nevertheless considered to be of special interest by reference to the same four features ie flora, fauna, geological or physiographical features. It is in this instance that the Natural Environmental Research Council (NERC) has to give an opinion on the merits and special interest of some of these features, though in practice, that Council and the Nature Conservancy Council at Peterborough work very closely together.

The NERC was set up by Royal Charter in 1965 and given its powers at the same time by the Science and Technology Act 1965. These are:

1 To protect the features in question by entering into an agreement with the relevant landowner by which he would refrain from exercising normal rights over that land eg ploughing.

2 The Council can pay recompense to the landowner for accepting this restraint.

3 In so far as the agreement then acts as a restrictive covenant, as described in Chapter 3, the law provides that the Council can enforce the agreement as if it were, in law, a neighbouring owner and thus able to enforce such a covenant to protect his own land (Countryside Act 1968 section 15). This technical legal provision is reinforced by forbidding the general law, under which courts can modify restrictive covenants, to apply to such agreements as we are now describing.

4 The Countryside Act 1968 includes another supporting power (section 32), whereby a Traffic Regulation Order can be made to control traffic movement eg parking, near to one of these SSSI.

It should also be noted that protection for areas of special scientific interest is also afforded under the Wildlife and Countryside Act 1981 (sections 28–33).

Notes

1 Act of 1968 section 1.
2 Act of 1949 sections 51–57.
3 Act of 1968 section 12.
4 Act of 1949 part V.
5 *See* Chapter 2 – Wildlife protection.
6 Act of 1968 section 30.

8.5 The British Tourist Authority

The British Tourist Authority (BTA) was established by the Development of Tourism Act 1966, which also set up the English, Scottish and Welsh Tourist Boards. The Board of the BTA is constituted by six persons appointed by the Secretary of State for Trade and Industry and the three chairmen of the above national Boards.

It has not been found necessary to amend this Act, which deals in Part I with the constitution and powers of the British Tourist Authority and the three national Boards and in Part II with financial assistance for hotel development. We limit this account to the legal powers and duties of the authority and leave questions of policy and financial grant to other books in this series.

The three national Boards consist of a chairman and six other persons, all appointed by the relevant Secretary of State (section 1).

The Act expands on the ways in which the Authority may discharge its functions by listing the promotion of publicity, the provision of information and advisory services, research and assisting financially other organisations by reimbursing their expenditure on items which the Authority would itself do. These could well include the Countryside Commission, the National Trust and local authorities.

Objects

The prime function of the British Tourist Authority and the three national Boards is to encourage people to visit Great Britain and also to encourage the islanders to take their own holidays here. The second object is to encourage the provision and improvement of tourist amenities in Great Britain.

The three main current means by which these aims are advanced are financial aid via the three national Boards, schemes of hotel development and, thirdly, promotion by local authorities.[1] We turn to each of these briefly.

Tourist Board financial aid
The BTA may prepare schemes under the above Act to give financial assistance to carry out schemes to fulfil the above statutory objects. This help may take the form of a grant or a loan or a combination of these methods. The procedure is for such a scheme to go to the Department of Trade and Industry for approval, which is by Order. Other forms of financial help can include taking shares in a company incorporated in Great Britain.[2]

Hotel development
Loans and grants for hotel development can be made by the three national Tourist Boards. They have to be subject to conditions laid down by the minister.

Local authorities
Local authorities have legal powers to stimulate tourism. Section 144 of the Local Government Act 1972 shows the wide range contemplated: 'Encourage persons by advertisement or otherwise, to visit their area for recreation,

for health purposes, or to hold conferences, trade fairs and exhibitions in their area and provide and improve facilities for these purposes'. This promotion work may be done alone or jointly with another person. Local authorities also have the important power to contribute to organisations established to encourage persons to visit the United Kingdom.

The British Tourist Authority and its Boards are a hive of activity and this account of legal powers does not begin to move into the colourful area of promotion schemes, which are the lifeblood of their work. An annual report gives more of that flavour.

We have been looking only at the legal framework and powers of the various bodies whose resources can greatly help leisure services management. This necessarily hides the colour and indeed prestige due to some by the large productions they can promote or assist. It does however underline the restrictions, whether by Charter or Statute, which affect the way they all operate. This means that all could be challenged for acting *ultra vires* in an extreme case, in addition to their submission to normal accounting controls.

Notes

1 A glance at a recent annual report of the BTA will show details of promotions at embassies all over the world and other exhibitions and schemes equally far flung. This text confines itself to the UK legal situation.
2 Act of 1969 section 4. There is greater detail in the companion volume in this series *Economics and Leisure Services Management*. Particulars of individual schemes are in the three national Boards' reports.

8.6 The Arts Council

This body was established by Royal Charter in 1946. Its objects are to develop and improve the knowledge, understanding and practice of the arts, to increase the accessibility of the arts to the public throughout Great Britain and to cooperate with government departments, local authorities and other bodies to achieve these ends.

The Council consists of a chairman and not more than eighteen other persons. An assessor who works with the Council is appointed by the Secretary of State for Education and Science, who also appoints the chairman.

There is also a Welsh Council, with interlocking membership and a Scottish Arts Council, whose chairman is a member of the British Arts Council.

We confine ourselves necessarily to the legal aspect of this Council's work and so mention that there are twelve regional Arts Councils through which the central Arts Council works.

The leisure services manager, interested in Arts Council support for, say, a special concert, would thus turn initially to his regional Arts Council. Only if the project had national overtones would he normally find himself dealing with the Central Council.

As the arts cover many fields, the Council has set up specialist advisory panels on individual arts or groups of arts. These sift and scrutinise applications for help, in order to discourage and dissuade the eccentric and encourage the genuine.

Conclusion

Until English law is codified, it must appear uneven to those who meet it for the first time. Sometimes it is said that cases go to court because the parties do not agree that the law is clear in relation to the facts of their problem. The attitude of the 'reasonable man', the correspondence of a sample with the bulk supply, the fitness of an appliance for its purpose, the suitability of development of a special kind in a special setting within the criteria laid down in the Town and Country Planning Acts – each of these everyday legal questions can give rise to two different opinions. We trust we have given a sufficient outline of first principles and problem areas in leisure services law to allow readers to sympathise with a famous lawyer, Lord Mansfield, who said: 'Most of the disputes in the world arise from words'.[1]

Note

1 *Morgan v Jones* (1773) Ftnt. Lofft 160.

Further reading

Chapter 1

Abel-Smith B, Stevens R 1970 *Lawyers and the Courts*. Heinemann.
Geldart W 1984 *Introduction to English Law*. Oxford University Press.
Harris P 1984 *An Introduction to Law*. Weidenfeld and Nicolson.

Chapter 2

Cross C A 1981 *Principles of Local Government Law*. Sweet and Maxwell.
Cullingworth J B 1972 *Town and Country Planning in Britain*. Geo Allen
   and Unwin.
Scott M 1985 *Law of Public Leisure Services*. Sweet and Maxwell.
Telling A E 1986 *Planning Law and Procedure*. Butterworths.

Chapter 3

Baker C D 1981 *Tort*. Sweet and Maxwell.
Green E F, Henderson N 1980 *Land Law*. Sweet and Maxwell.
Hogan B *et al* 1981 *A-Level Law*. Sweet and Maxwell.

Chapter 4

Bowers, J 1986 *A Practical Approach to Employment Law*. Financial Train-
   ing Publications Limited.
Fleming J G 1983 *The Law of Torts*. Sweet and Maxwell.
Palmer C, Poulton K 1987 *Sex and Race Discrimination in Employment*.
   Legal Action Group.
Selwyn H 1982 *Law of Health and Safety at Work*. Butterworths.

Chapter 5

Anson 1984 *Anson's Law of Contract.* Clarendon.
Hardy Ivamy E R 1984 *Casebook on Insurance Law.* Butterworths.
Leigh N H, Joffe V H, Goldberg D 1987 *Introduction to Company Law.* Butterworths.
Nelson-Jones R, Stewart P 1987 *Product Liability.* Fourmat Publishing.
Savage N, Bradgate R 1987 *Business Law.* Butterworths.

Chapter 6

Smith C M, Monkcom S P 1987 *Law of Betting, Gaming and Lotteries.* Butterworths.

Chapter 7

Hayton D J 1980 *Cases and Commentary on the Law of Trusts.* Steven and Sons.
Keeton G W *The Law of Trusts.* Pitman.

Chapter 8

Annual reports of the bodies in question.
Hughes D 1986 *Environmental Law.* Butterworths.

Index